# GRANDFATHER MOUNTAIN

## A PROFILE

*By*

*Miles Tager*

Parkway Publishers, Inc.
Boone, North Carolina

1999

*Library of Congress Cataloging-in-Publication Data:*

Tager, Miles.
    Grandfather Mountain : a profile / by Miles Tager.
            p.     cm.
    Includes bibliographical references and index.
    ISBN 1-887905-17-0
    1.  Grandfather Mountain (N.C.) --History. 2.
Grandfather Mountain (N.C.) --Description and travel. 3.  Natural
History--North Carolina--Grandfather Mountain. I. Title.
    F262.B6T34    1999
    975.6'862--dc21
                                                            99-25202
                                                                CIP

*Cover Design By Bill May, Jr.*
*Photo Layout By Aaron Burleson*

*Editing, layout and book design by Julie Shissler*

# Contents

*Foreword*

*Preface*

*Introduction*

*Glossary*

## *Origins*
Rock. . . . . . . . . . . . . . . . 1
Life. . . . . . . . . . . . . . . .11
    Flora. . . . . . . . . . . . .12
    Fauna. . . . . . . . . . . .27
Humans. . . . . . . . . . . .53

## *Growth*
Explorations. . . . . . . .67
Explanations. . . . . . . .77

## *Developments*
Exploitation. . . . . . . .85
Preservation. . . . . . . .89

*Index*

## Foreword

As you head south from the town of Banner Elk on Highway 184 you run into a mountain. Grandfather Mountain, to be exact. It doesn't sneak up on you; you see it coming from a distance. When you get to the end of the highway, you have several choices if you want to get to its other side. You can head west several miles until you come to the Yohnalossee Road that skirts the flank of the mountain. Or you can head east several miles and head down windy old Shull's Mill Road.

My personal favorite, however, is to go over the mountain, on foot. As you start out, the trail runs along a stream that forms the headwaters of the Watauga River, one of the many streams that Grandfather spawns. You then gradually proceed up the mountain, through shady coves carpeted with wildflowers, gnarly stands of rhododendron and a bounty of songbirds.

Eventually the forest changes, turning into an evergreen forest of Fraser Firs and Red Spruces. The animals change too, as evidenced by the frenetic song of the winter wren. Turn over a rock and you might be introduced to a Weller's salamander, a creature of golden beauty. This is clearly a strange place, inhabited by tiny tarantulas and rock gnome lichens. If you happen to be in this forest when the clouds roll in (not an unusual occurrence) you almost expect a gnome or at least a fairy to appear in the mist.

Finally, after ascending some 2,000 feet you arrive at Calloway Peak, at 5,964 feet the highest of the rocky peaks of Grandfather. The view is outstanding. To the south the slopes of Grandfather sink down into the green sea of the Pisgah National Forest, while to the north, Grandfather's close kin, Hanging Rock, looms. As you descend the south side of the mountain, you hit the "Cragway", yet another Grandfather community -- a dry, shrubby, heath habitat , with cliffs of ancient sandstone covered with sand myrtle, no less.

Ultimately, the lush deciduous forest returns and you find yourself on the Blue Ridge Parkway. This is not the base of the mountain, however. Indeed, the mountain continues to descend another 2,000 feet into the forested coves and ridges of the

Wilson Creek, Little Lost Cove Creek and Harper Creek watersheds, and to the very edge of the Appalachians.

The story of this mountain, hoever, involves more than ancient rocks and forests. It seems that people have been visiting this mountain for quite a while for different reasons. We know that the Cherokee called it *Tanawha* as well as home. And Andre Michaux, the intrepid French botanist, while collecting plants on Grandfather, found the majesty of the mountain so overwhelming that the sedate Frenchman broke into song. But in the early 20th century the tidal wave of timber harvesting that had cleared out the northern forests swept in and Grandfather found its slopes devastated. Since that time, the slopes have recovered only to be set upon by their latest nemesis, recreational development.

The beauty of this book is that it tells the whole story of the mountain, from rocks to salamanders to Daniel Boone and beyond. The author shows us that we cannot ignore the human impact on the mountain any more than we can ignore its rich biodiversity... that the key to preserving Grandfather's future lies in understanding its past. That Grandfather Mountain is the heart of this part of the Appalachians we call home, and that its future is our future.

Read this book and then climb "The Grandfather." Then, you will understand.

*Stewart Skeate, Ph.D.*
*June, 1999*

*Preface*

December, 1993 - North Slope of Grandfather Mountain.

The storm had passed the night before, leaving four inches of fresh snow, the first of the season. Once across the Watauga River, rolling and tumbling so near its pristine source on the Continental Divide, the trail began, and from there rose like a white carpet to the heavens. The heavens on this morning ached with the purest blue of the imagination.

After an hour, we had approached the 5,000 ft. mark, leaving the deep mixed hardwood forest for the evergreens dotting the exposed rocky shoulder up to the summit. With the Spruce-fir and Balsam etching the horizon, the vista opened to show the entire sweep of the North Slope; river and meadow, cove and crag.

From this point to the ridge, we stopped to see every tree shine in the stillness of the morning light; the sun dancing off the coating of crystal rime frost. Below the looming Profile Cliff, home to Peregrine and legendary eagle Tanawha, we reach our goal; the Crystal Mine, a quartz outcropping thirty feet high perched on Grandfather's shoulder. Powder snow, glistening ice, and now shining rock. The silence, serenity, and expanse of mountain seem equally without limit.

We hear no sound.

No question; it is here in the High Country of North Carolina, not the Alps or the Rockies, that we have hiked the most stunning mountain trail of our lives.

Everyone cherishes an intense relationship with a place. My bond with the Grandfather Mountain, although unique, is also shared with thousands that have come before, to explore it, enjoy it, protect it, and honor it in writing. The mountain is big enough for all who come there to take home something for their own. This narrative, I hope, will take into account that attraction between human and mountain, a relationship no less mysterious and compelling than between human and human.

I also hope that all those that deserve special mention in this context will recognize themselves in the text of this book, but the following friends and forerunners must be credited, and acknowledged for their critical roles in helping to preserve the mountain, the manuscript, and in some cases the writer himself. Thanks then, in equal order of importance, to Harlan Kelsey, the Grandfather's greatest advocate, who lost his ultimate battle to completely preserve his most beloved place, but never lost his integrity or will.

Thanks to scientists Dr. Matt Roe and Wayne Van Devender of Appalachian State University for their assistance; also ASU's Dr. Loren Raymond and Dr. Harvard Ayers for tackling an amateur's foray into their fields, and scientist Dr. Stewart Skeate of Lees McRae College for all of the above, a fine critical eye, and friendship.

Also: state archaeologist David Moore and the efficient folks at the Appalachian Collection in Boone.

Special thanks, kudos, and appreciation to Richard Jackson, Lees-McRae College Librarian; Aaron Burleson for his photo layouts; Grandfather Mountain, Inc.'s Jim Morton; Julie Shissler, editor and book designer; and Bill May, Jr., cover designer.

One group of individuals must take center stage in the formation of this book, for without them I would not have come to know, research, and joyously obsess about the Grandfather Mountain for five years. I would not have moved to within a mile of the North Slope, met my wife, held my current job.

In 1989, when I received the phone call, I had never seen the mountain, although at the time was living only a few hours away.

"Do you know what they are planning to do on Grandfather?" the woman asked. I had no idea, but within a week was traveling frozen January backroads -- lost in darkest Plumtree! -- to meet for the first time The Grandfather Mountain and the folks trying to stop a thousand-acre development on his North Slope. That event would change many lives, but none more than my own.

Special thanks, then to the Friends of Grandfather Mountain: Martha Stephenson, Conley Stegall, Kevin Balling, Dan Woodend, and Pam Scarborough.

Special Friends indeed.

*For Tristan*

# Introduction

This book is about one of the world's great mountains, the Grandfather Mountain of North Carolina. To see it for yourself, step out of your car along the Blue Ridge Parkway in northwestern North Carolina, and look up. Grandfather's multiple summits and jutting tors, the long chiseled ridgetop fringed with fragrant balsam stand out among the subtle and graduated slopes of this High Country like the craggy patriarch of an ancient clan.

As indeed he is. Created millions of centuries ago, the Grandfather Mountain is one of the oldest peaks in the Blue Ridge Mountains. Viewed from any angle, the massif has weathered these millennia in peerless form.

All his notable Appalachian compatriots, Mount Mitchell and the Blacks, Craggy Dome, Roan Mountain, Guyot and Clingman's Dome in the Great Smokies, stand taller. Their framework has been beaten down by the battering of wind, water, and ice into the definitive rounded brows and forested shoulders so characteristic of the southern mountains. Grandfather's escarpment stands alone, jutting 4,000 ft. out of the Piedmont Plain below, an elevation gain that creates the visual dominance equal to the much higher peaks of the American West.

Such fine framework has laid the foundation for an equally remarkable biological development. Settled in a nurturing temperate clime (albeit disturbed by the occasional natural cataclysm), the mountain grew a natural treasure trove of flora and fauna unparalleled in the hemisphere's mid-latitudes. Grandfather's diverse habitats support more rare and endangered species and communities than any other mountain east of the Rockies, more indeed than a majority of states in the union. The mountain is internationally recognized as a haven for rare lichen, mosses, flowering herbs, trees, salamanders, birds, and mammals.

The Grandfather's history parallels the evolution of the Blue Ridge, one of the most biologically diverse ranges of mountains on earth. It is a microcosm of an organic weave so intricate and so intertwined that these mountains have been called "a single giant organism."

Grandfather Mountain is the fractal-like heart of the Appalachian mosaic, a perfect miniature of the whole intricate pattern; and the crown jewel of one of the richest biomes on the planet. The abundance and variety of life here have from the beginning attracted considerable human attention. The forebears of the Cherokee bestowed on this entity the name of their ascendant spirit; Tanawha, the Fabulous Eagle.

Grandfather's great cliffs, rivers and forests were places of extraordinary mythic power and practical value alike, two aspects, like the twin lenses of binoculars, indistinguishable in the Native American view. The mountain yielded spirits, totems, legends and lore; and crystal, stone, fiber, wood, bark, game, fish, herbs, and medicine.

For ten thousand years, nomadic Indians came and went in seasonal flux, took what they needed, but disturbed little on the mountain. With the coming of the European colonists, Grandfather's virgin wilderness felt for the first time the bite of the saw and bark of the musket.

But the earliest explorers and pioneers, Daniel Boone prominent among them, were disinclined to tame the wild. Unlike the Pilgrims, who viewed nature as the devil's work, the first settlers in southern Appalachia eagerly sought the solace and splendor of the mountain forest. Teeming with flocks and herds that rustled giant ferns under the canopy of two-hundred-foot high trees, the sweep of Grandfather Mountain and its possibilities must have been wonders to behold.

For a century or so, the isolation and rugged conditions kept all but the hardiest souls at bay. The small hunting parties, scientific expeditions, and rough settlements of single room log cabins did little to change the life of, and on, Grandfather as it had evolved for millennia.

Then just two hundred years ago, or one-millionth of the mountain's life-span, the modern era clanged on steel rails into the remote coves of the Grandfather and the Blue Ridge, changing both forever. Some of the changes the industrial revolution wrought are obvious: some invisible, some permanent, some reversible.

In recent times the mountain has drawn focus as a prime example of both reckless devastation, and nature's astonishing powers, given a chance, of regeneration. Even now, surrounded by talismans of development strewn along his and surrounding slopes, Grandfather survives as a geological and biological centerpiece unique in the Appalachians and the world , a living, if fragile, eminence.

And so I have called this book a profile.

This mountain rewards all vantage points; scientific, historical, cultural, spiritual, and visual. We will explore them all; from the first birth cry of colliding rock plates to the stillness of the salamander hidden now, possibly just feet away, in a stream pool.

We will hear the trill of warbler amidst a flurry of flame azalea; stalk with Neolithic hunting bands, sojourn with biologists, renegades, adventurers, hermits, herbalists, and modern spirit seekers, as we follow the many paths of the mountain.

Stand today on a crag overlooking a high heath bald, and watch the sun flash off the rock as it is shot through with crystal quartz. Then descend into the quiet of the dark coves, dense with moss, fern, trillium and ancient secrets. Look up through the forest canopy for the Peregrine falcons along the profile of the sleeping ancient, the wind-carved face of the old man that gives the mountain its name.

Or you can just listen to the old-timers, who know. Along the Watauga River in the Grandfather Community, or down Wilson's Creek to Roseborough, or up at Boone's Fork, you can find someone to tell you, simply, how special is this mountain. Ask them for directions and they'll sum it up. They'll say, that's the way, up there, to the Grandfather. Not Grandfather Mountain, mind you, but The Grandfather.

A grand old man; a great mountain.

# Distribution of Forest Types
## by Slope Exposure and Elevation

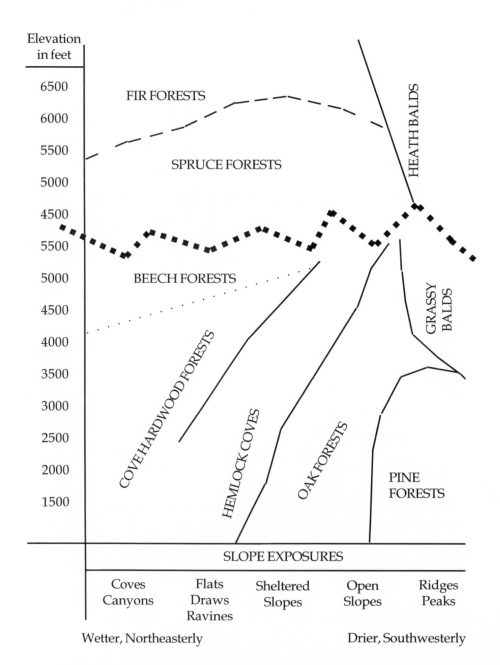

(Adapted from R.H. Whittaker, 1956. "Vegetation of the Great Smoky Mountains"
Ecological Monographs, *Vol 26, No 1, p.58)*

# Glossary

*Biomes* A complex of communities characterized by a distinctive type of vegetation and maintained under the climatic conditions of the region.

*Boreal* Of or pertaining to the north; northern.

*Efflux* Outward flow, as of water.

*Endemic* Peculiar to a particular people or locality; indigenous.

*Escarpment* A long, precipitous, clifflike ridge of land, rock, or the like, commonly formed by faulting or fracturing of the earth's crust.

*Igneous* Produced under conditions involving intense heat, as rocks of volcanic origin.

*Massif* A compact portion of a mountain range, containing one or more summits.

*Mast* The fruit of the oak, beech or other forest trees, used as food for animals.

*Mesic* Of or pertaining to or adapted to an environment having a balanced supply of moisture.

*Mesophytic* A plant growing best under conditions of well-balanced moisture.

*Passerines* Of, belonging to or pertaining to order *Passeriformes,* comprising more than half of all birds, and typically having feed adapted for perching.

*Relict* A plant or animal species living in an environment which has changed from that which is typical for it.

*Talus* A sloping mass of rocky fragments at the base of a cliff.

*Tectonic* Pertaining to the structure of the earth's crust.

*Tors* A rocky pinnacle; a peak of a bare or rocky mountain or hill.

*Ungulate* Having hooves; the group comprising all hooved animals.

*Vugs* A small cavity in a rock or lode, often lined with crystals.

# GEOLOGIC TIME SCALE

| SYSTEM AND PERIOD | | SERIES AND EPOCH | SOME DISTINCTIVE FEATURES | YEARS BEFORE PRESENT |
|---|---|---|---|---|
| CENOZOIC | QUATERNARY | RECENT | Modern man | 11 thousand |
| | | PLEISTOCENE | Early man; northern glaciation | 1/2 to 2 million |
| | | | | 13 +/- 1 million |
| | TERTIARY | PLIOCENE | Large carnivores | 25 +/- 1 million |
| | | MIOCENE | First abundant grazing mammals | |
| | | OLIGOCENE | Large running mammals | 36 +/- 2 million |
| | | EOCENE | Many modern types of mammals | 58 +/- 2 million |
| | | PALEOCENE | First placental mammals | 63 +/- 2 million |
| MESOZOIC | CRETACEOUS | | First flowering plants; climax of dinosaurs and ammonites, followed by extinction | 135 +/- 5 million |
| | JURASSIC | | First birds, first mammals; dinosaurs and ammonites abundant | 181 +/- 5 million |
| | TRIASSIC | | First dinosaurs, abundant cycads and conifers | 230 +/- 10 million |
| PALEOZOIC | PERMIAN | | Extinction of many kinds of marine animals, including trilobites. Southern glaciation | 280 +/- 10 million |
| | CARBONIFEROUS | PENNSYLVANIAN | Great coal forests, conifers. First reptiles | 310 +/- 10 million |
| | | MISSISSIPPIAN | Sharks and amphibians abundant. Large and numerous scale trees and seed ferns | 345 +/- 10 million |
| | DEVONIAN | | First amphibians and ammonites; fishes abundant | 405 +/- 10 million |
| | SILURIAN | | First terrestrial plants and animals | 425 +/- 10 million |
| | ORDOVICIAN | | First fishes; invertebrates dominant | 500 +/- 10 million |
| | CAMBRIAN | | First abundant record of marine life; trilobites dominant | 600 +/- 50 million |
| PRECAMBRIAN | | | Fossils extremely rare, consisting of promitive aquatic plants. Evidence of glaciation. Oldest dated algae, over 2600 million years; oldest dated meteorites 4500 million years | |

Maurice Brooks, *The Appalachians* (Boston: Houghton Mifflin, 1965), p.14.

# CHAPTER 1

## *Rock*

Grandfather Mountain was born underground a billion years ago; its oldest rock granites formed in a titanic collision of moving continents.

On the surface of the earth, wind alone moved the waters and broke the silence. No creature swam or bird flew. During the four billion years of these Precambrian times only the most primitive ancestors of our current organisms and ecosystems existed. Primitive algae ruled the natural world.

Life was evolving with incomprehensible patience; the algae had formed one and a half billion years earlier, and the first shimmer of fish was still 500 million years away.

Below the surface, the earth's crust was shifting restlessly, impelled by heat, pressure, and sedimentation, squeezed between the crust above, the mantle and then the molten core beneath. Sandstones and shales were laid down in sheets, with granite forced up through the violent tectonic shifts. During the almost half a million millennia of the Precambrian era, these conflicting forces metamorphosed the rock and salt and sand and shell into an aggregate composed of pebbles of quartz, slate, shale, granite, rhyolite, and other volcanic materials, ultimately becoming a massive solid matrix.

Grandfather Mountain lay waiting for birth.

At the beginning of the Paleozoic era, the latest of the Phanerozoic Eon (the largest unit of geologic time), a giant trough was ground out of the crust along the present line of the Appalachian Mountains. Like clay into a mold, sedimentary material packed in to the depression.

The great mountain building formations began in the region, literally in shock waves, in the early Paleozoic, between 440 and 500 million years ago. Further uprooting continued through the era; 100 million years later and again, and most significantly, 300 million years ago.

The seas were now brimming with life, first microorganisms, then protozoa, trilobites, later invertebrates and fish. As the mountains were elevated, many of the more advanced forms of sea life were forced to rapidly adapt themselves to existence on the new landscape.

The Appalachian conglomerate beds nesting in their trough lay atop one of the largest land mass, or tectonic, plates that make up the earth's crust, the one that would in fact 'create' North America. The planet's core is molten and thereby fluid, as is the mantle below the earth's surface, and the rigid plates -- 70 to 160 miles thick -- were thought to be dragged together by the motion below and above.

As they move, tectonic plates can, and do, collide. Earthquakes, those shattering dislocations along the cracks in these plates, are the merest murmur compared to the cataclysm generated by this impact. When the North American plate ran aground, shearing and crumpling along a northeast/southwest incline, the resulting force thrust bedrock upward along a two-thousand mile chain from Alabama to Quebec. Due to the deep mass of metamorphosed stone underneath, the epicenter of this uplift created the highest peaks and ridges along a series of crests from what is currently east Tennessee to south Virginia, and along the entire length of western North Carolina.

The incoming plate appears to have been of later construction and to have ground over the Precambrian strata. Throughout the southern mountain region, most of the exposed rock formations date from Cambrian times or later, that is material no older than 600 million years before the present (B.P.). The exception is Roan Mountain, forty miles from Grandfather on the North Carolina-Tennessee border, with rock dated from 1,700 million years ago. Grandfather's oldest lava flows date to 740 million years ago. The oldest recorded formations on earth go back almost four billion years.

This last great mountain building event was called the Alleghenian Orogeny, and involved the plates containing Europe and Africa, and North America.

It was the slowly applied horizontal pressure of the tectonic movement, as opposed to a sudden volcanic thrust, that produced the characteristic folding and wrinkling on Appalachian slopes; the alternating ridge and valley aspect visible at any overlook in these mountains. Erosion may have softened the lines, but the overall contours seen today were formed during the rigors of birth. No one knows how high were the great peaks of this range.

Estimates vary from Himalayan heights, over twenty-five thousand feet on down, with more of a consensus toward Sierran altitudes in the ten to fifteen thousand foot category. There is little hard evidence either way.

The general uplifting continued into the Mesozoic Era, about 200 million years ago, when contact between the plates was evidently broken off. For a period of perhaps 150 million years the mountains slowly evolved, eroded, and wore down. Finally, a last push is thought to have occurred at the beginning of the Cenozoic Period, perhaps 60 million years ago, when the entire length of the chain may have lifted by as much as 4,000 feet.

In this largely uniform sequence of regional development, one anomaly would create a unique geologic design, a design that completed the formation of Grandfather Mountain. During either one of the groundbreaking collisions, or in an eruption all its own, the older Precambrian conglomerate was driven up in a solid slab of stone, in places overlaying the original rock formation; time turned on its head.

So exposed, this older stratum was eventually discovered, analyzed, and dated. It has been labeled the Grandfather Window, as one might think of a window to the origins of geologic time; an eroded opening in the rock mass that affords a view to earlier formations.

As the surrounding Blue Ridge continued to erode through the millennia, Grandfather's metamorphosed aggregate stood fast. Although readily visible as high elevation outcroppings of quartz streaked granite, many traces of the window are virtually indistinguishable from later deposits, and are easily and frequently overlooked. A case in point are the huge boulders of Wilson Creek Gneiss, which may be the oldest rock on the mountain. Only a short hike from the Blue Ridge Parkway along Wilson Creek on the Tanawha Trail, these massive stones are weatherbeaten and moss-covered and don't look to the casual observer particularly different than adjacent framework half its age.

One spectacular remnant, however, does loom large. On an exposed shoulder of the north slope at about 5,200 feet juts a great chunk of veined quartz thirty feet high.

As a fracture in the mountain opened during the mountain's metamorphism, the gap filled with fluid, laying in the deposit of quartz.

Within the vugs and matrix of the vein quartz sparkle geodes and gem quality crystals. Strewn at its feet tumbles a scree slope of more quartz, pebble to boulder size, no one knows how deep. Known locally as the crystal mine, this outcropping mirrors what some think is the window's, and possibly the mountain's, core. Speculation persists locally that somewhere at the heart of Grandfather exists a vast crystal cave, though scientists dispute any factual basis for such a phenomenon. Certainly there is nothing comparable on the surface of this or any other Blue Ridge peak.

The stratigraphy, or horizontal layering, of the window overlay is also clearly visible at the very southern end of Grandfather's south slope. Here roars Linville Falls, and here through the waters of the upper falls one can view in cross-section an upside-down layer cake. The falls plunge over a shelf of so-called Cranberry Gneiss, the most ancient building block lying directly on top of rock half a billion years younger.

The Window thrust was followed by at least two other events in the geo-formation of the region. Some 300 million years ago another ultimate collision occurred between the North American plate and the land mass that was destined to become the African continent. This impact was different than the first, with the plates not aggregating but crashing, ever so slowly of course, head on. This incident also took a little while -- about fifty million years or so -- but was, to date at least, final.

The two continents split for good, or rather for the extended moment, and allowed an ocean to form between them at about the time of the coming of the dinosaur.

Sometime during this Alleghany Orogeny period a particular tectonic shift or earthquake rumbled at the base of the mountain along, possibly creating the Linville Falls Fault. This lay the groundwork for the Linville River Gorge, now a 2,000 foot plunge from the mountain's east slope, one of the deepest canyons in the eastern United States and a renowned wilderness area.

For all its antiquity, it would be wrong to consider Grandfather's geological development as entirely a thing of the past, one that has stopped emerging. Most of the primal forces that fashioned him -- wind, water, and the weathering of the seasons -- are still active. The changes wrought are inestimably gradual, and the occasional cataclysms eons apart, but the mountain -- like all mountains -- does not remain in some dormant state, but is always changing. Geologic, climatic, and organic developments are often undetectable in our short lifetimes, but they are no less dramatic for that.

During the Pleistocene Era, the time of animal and then human domain lasting from two million to ten thousand years ago, an upheaval thousands of miles to the north of the Blue Ridge range nevertheless altered these mountains forever. Loosed from the north, vast sheets of glacial ice plowed down the eastern seaboard, stopping in a line from the Ohio Valley to Long Island. New York State's Adirondack Mountains, the northernmost reach of the Appalachian chain, were likely buried under a five to seven mile-thick coat of ice. This last great North American ice age drove every temperate species before it, profoundly altering the ecological balance of all southeastern bio-regions, but especially the Appalachians.

So great were the changes wrought that scientists have long pondered the possibility that the ice actually penetrated into the South. In 1973, certain indications persuaded two North Carolina geologists to publicly postulate that local mountain glaciers had in fact formed on the higher Appalachian peaks 15,000 years ago. The proof, they said, was on Grandfather Mountain.

Published in a prestigious national scientific journal, their theory cited thirty to forty parallel grooves in the metamorphic rock on Grandfather's northeast slope. These striations appeared to match those in the Adirondacks and elsewhere that were the tell-tale signature of glacial grinding. Along with other secondary signs such as the slope's numerous boulderfields, talus slopes, polished bedrock, and whaleback rock formations, the researchers felt this evidence was not only conclusive, but "irrefutable".

True, the complete lack of true fossil remains ( exact molds or reproductions of animal or vegetable remains that have imprinted by various means on a natural element) meant there could be no absolute physical confirmation, but at least their absence did not necessarily refute the other evidence. These forms can imprint on a number of surfaces including sedimentary rock, but do not and cannot occur in the hard volcanic matrix of the Appalachians.

This announcement, and publication of the findings, brought international headlines and acclaim. There were critical and far-reaching ramifications in research fields from botany to oceanography; in fact, the entire natural history of the southeast United States would have to be reexamined in light of this discovery.

The theoretical bubble floated happily aloft for a number of months. That is, until an old-timer living near the mountain decided to take a look at photographs of those rock grooves. They reminded him, in fact, they looked exactly like, the deep cuts made by the logging chains scraping over the rock as they had skidded the big trees during the clear-cutting of the mountain in the 1930's. Despite subsequent weeks of dodging the bullet, the balloon had been exploded; the marks were man-made and there existed no irrefutable evidence that glaciers had ground over Grandfather Mountain or anywhere else south of the accepted line across the Northeast United States.

The immediate impact of the Adirondack glaciation on Grandfather and other high southern peaks was secondary to longer term changes caused by both the initial climate change and the slow subsequent warm-up that followed their return north to the arctic. Species living at elevations above 5,000 ft. were driven along with the tree line down to 3,000 ft. The different vegetation 'zones', and the animals that depended on them had been compressed not only along the lower elevations but were pushed compass south in order to survive the cold spell intact.

Above that 3,000 ft. elevation, sub-arctic tundra reigned. The wave of refugee flora and fauna fleeing the ice radically changed the life of the mountain forever, and set the stage for its current form.

For the last sixty million years of the Cenozoic period until the present time, best evidence suggests that the great dynamics determining the shape of Grandfather Mountain were now being provided by the myriad elements of erosion. This array of seemingly destructive, seasonally recurring forces -- gale force winds, deluge, ice, and cold -- played the last crucial part in creating today's configuration.

Although difficult to pinpoint exactly, Grandfather Mountain stands now over ten miles long, three miles wide, and between 2,500 and 6,000 ft. high, an area of approximately 150 square miles, or about 100,000 acres. For those accustomed to thinking only of the summit area as 'the' mountain, it comes as something of a shock to consider this arena, slopes stretching from Linville Gorge to Julian Price Park, from the Watauga River etching the base of the north slope to Wilson's Creek sweeping down to Brown Mountain and the Piedmont plain, as being all Grandfather Mountain.

No one can say how, or how much this massif has modified over eons of battering from the elements. But it is safe to say that the Grandfather Mountain window has stood as the proverbial immovable object over time's irresistible force, and that its size and shape may be closer to its ancient form than any other southern mountain.

The unique geological composition has made The Grandfather an anomaly in one other important regard as well. Standing in the midst of one of the country's richest gem and commercial mineral areas, within a few hours' drive of an astonishing variety of valuable veins and deposits, Grandfather Mountain's impermeable core has yielded few precious stones.

Ruby, sapphire, emerald, garnet, amethyst, tourmaline, beryl, and over fifty other gemstones are actively mined in the vicinity, including some of the largest discovered anywhere in the world. Commercially, the Spruce Pine-High Country area has been mined for gold, iron, zinc, mica, kaolin, feldspar, lead, copper, and manganese as well as greenstone, slate and other prized building stone. Large ironworks at Cranberry and mica mining in adjacent Mitchell County attest to the wealth of valuable material still available at Grandfather's doorstep.

Yet almost no saleable gems or minerals have been found on the mountain itself. Only relatively insignificant veins of gold, which can still be panned from nearby streams, were uncovered in three shafts opened on the mountain during the early 1800's. Some of the rich quartz veins, the one mineral Grandfather has in abundance, showed some gold-bearing pyrite, but insufficient to encourage serious mining. Crystalline quartz is itself limited in commercial value to the manufacture of oscillator plates for the electronics industry, and is of course readily available in many other more accessible locations.

Some quarrying was done for 'Grandfather Stone', a light grey-green building stone, but again the abundance of other fine material from gentler locales -- and more stringent Federal permitting -- discouraged massive quarrying among the mountain's steep slopes and choked ravines.

Prospectors hunted uranium here in the 1950's but left empty-handed.

The lithological forces that caused the Window and shaped Grandfather in a different cast than the surrounding mineral-rich lands spared him numerous gross indignities. Both active and abandoned mines, pits, cuts, dumps and tailings litter the vicinity of Spruce Pine, only twenty-five miles distant, and would have devastated Grandfather's fragile natural beauty and diversity.

After the last ice pack receded to the Arctic, and life returned to the now temperate zones of the southern mountains, Grandfather's stunning range of habitat attracted a host of species and communities. Up on the exposed ridgetops and in the sheltered coves, down the 3,500 foot inclines and throughout the watersheds of the rivers and branches, a plethora of flora rooted, flowered, reproduced and evolved.

During the next ten thousand years many flourished unimpeded, nourishing an equally rich menagerie of foraging and nesting creatures, both native and migrant.

As Grandfather Mountain entered the recent era, all the diverse elements of his past joined to produce a network of natural systems as singular, complete and interdependent as a living being, an individual masterpiece.

# CHAPTER 2

## *Life*

Grandfather Mountain encompasses several remarkable ecosystems. The largest, or macrocosmic framework is the Appalachian Mountain Range, encompassing every American peak east of the Mississippi. The southern Appalachians, distinguished by elevation and climate as well as latitude, include the mountains of Alabama, Georgia, Tennessee, Kentucky, the Virginias, and the Carolinas.

If the Appalachians are the rock ribs of eastern America, the Blue Ridge can be considered its spine, a narrow band stretching 615 miles from Carlisle, Pennsylvania to Mount Oglethorpe in Georgia, and by some reckoning into the hills of northern Alabama.

At their narrowest northpoint they are only five miles wide, and along their widest stretch in North Carolina still reach only sixty-five miles across. The Blue Ridge are one of the most ancient American mountains, forming at the end of the Cambrian era, then disjoining from other distinct eastern ranges, the Alleghanies, the Great Smokies, and the Black Mountains, during the folding and troughing of subsequent upheavals. Some recent scientific thinking considers the Blacks and other ranges as subdivisions of the Blue Ridge, which would make Mount Mitchell, the highest peak in the eastern United States, the highest Blue Ridge mountain as well. Like the others, they came to term through millennia of erosion that carved the innumerable river valleys, shadowy coves, and robust forests.

If no longer conclusively the highest and oldest peak in the Blue Ridge chain, as has frequently been claimed, Grandfather Mountain nevertheless dominates the region known as the North Carolina High Country, which includes the extreme northwestern counties of Ashe, Watauga, Avery, and Mitchell.

Although unique, Grandfather Mountain lives within this sequence of ecological systems as part of a region, a chain, and a range. It must therefore be recognized within all these parameters, belonging to a series of natural infrastructures that are distinct, yet interdependent. So complex and closely linked are the components of this far-reaching ecological community that they share some of the integral traits of human physiology; a systemic breakdown at any level affects the whole, and the other parts of the whole.

We are obliged, then, to view mountain chains in the precise meaning of the term; like the biological food chain or the links of nucleic acid that are the building blocks of life, their integrity can be compromised or even broken by the destruction of just one link.

Driven by many startling indications of system-wide failure in integrated systems throughout the world, modern science is scrambling to come to grips with the essence of this linkage, to determine how it works, and how to reverse the deterioration once it has reached such a critical juncture.

Much of their attention is now focused on the ancient uplands of the eastern United States, because few places exist on earth with more to preserve, or lose, than the Appalachians.

## *Flora*

More than two hundred years ago, botanist Andre Michaux observed a mountain forest in North Carolina that will never be seen again, and understood instinctively what later proved established fact; biologically the Appalachians are the richest temperate forest known to exist on earth. "The Appalachians are a forest upon a high rolling floor, and in all the continent, in all the world I believe, there is no such hardwood or deciduous forest as this...nothing bleak, nothing eroded, nothing arid...everywhere the murmur of leaves, the trickling or rushing of water." Even now, gravely injured and further threatened by human development, this range is noted by Audubon naturalists as the "zenith of forest development". ·

The Great Smoky Mountains alone contain more deciduous trees, and more tree species overall, than all the forests of Europe.

The so-called Cove Forests of the Smokies and Blue Ridge (those remaining few not logged) nestle in the protected bowls formed in the ancient folds, and can produce up to forty tree

species in one stand. These remaining stands of the original
ecosystem hold many North American record and near-record
tree species: Yellow Poplar (30 foot circumference), Yellow
Buckeye (16 feet), Eastern Hemlock (20 feet), Sugar Maple (13
feet), Yellow Birch (14 feet), Basswood, Mountain Silverbell,
White Ash, American Beech, Northern Red Oak, Black Cherry,
and Cucumber Tree.

The Southern Appalachians maintain over two hundred
species of hardwoods and over a hundred types of flowering
trees, both records for temperate woodlands. The oldest
surviving trees here have lived for over five hundred years.
Although most renowned for their deciduous species, the
southern mountain region spots fourteen varieties of native
conifers, including the Red Spruce and Fraser Fir, sub-alpine
and Canadian Tundra species that have graced the higher slopes
since the receding ice pack. The Red Spruce is in fact identical to
its northern forerunner, while the fir, or balsam as it is often
called in the South, has evolved into a separate species, a
curious development considering the two species are so closely
allied that they have formed their own ecosystem - the southern
Spruce-Fir Forest.

However, as conservationists are fond of saying, forests are
more than trees, and the Appalachian woodlands abound even
today in splendid multiformity. Look here for two hundred
species of wildflowers, four hundred species of mosses and
liverworts (primitive moss-like plants), two thousand species of
fungi and mushrooms: a greenhouse unparalleled beyond the
tropical rainforests.

The flip side of such long-standing diversity is systemic
integration, a natural order operating as that single giant
organism. If the innermost secrets of this process remain
mysterious, two simple facts can account for at least some of its
success; the region's half-billion year lifespan, and the equally
rare provision that those eons of evolution have been provided
to date free of cataclysmic turbulence.

Indications are that climatic as well as geologic conditions
have moderated in the last ten thousand years since the last ice
age. This has meant plentiful steady rainfall year round,

probably in today's range of 40 to 80 inches per year. Prevailing winds are westerly, drying the northern and western slopes, but leaving the lee sides, and the coves, to continually saturate with moisture. Steady rains, steady winds, and being the South, steady sunshine.

Within this framework, the vagaries of mountain weather (Grandfather Mountain has recorded both the highest winds -- 195 mph -- and the lowest mean temperature - minus 34 degrees Fahrenheit -- in not only the mountains but the state and the entire South), will have served to strengthen both the vitality and variety of life on the mountain. In these climes, temperatures fall by an average of 4-5 degrees F per thousand feet of elevation gain, more gradually than along the steeper, often sheer, gradients of the great mountains of the American West.

This range of favorable conditions already welcomed a myriad of plants and animals before the ice sheet ground southward one last time. When it stopped, roughly a thousand miles away, many species, with attendant seeds, spores, and pollen, had already fled south before it. They lodged in sheltered nooks on the higher slopes and ridges, deposited by the winds in some suitable locations mimicking their northern homes.

Some died, some adapted.

When the cold and ice began to recede and the climate moderated, the natural tendency was for many of the species that fled south to follow the warm-up back north.

But then a funny thing happened on the way home. Fooled by a high-altitude climate and conditions similar to the arboreal and sub-arctic terrain of New England and Canada, the northern endemic flora and fauna, from mosses to mammals, moved up the slopes of the higher southern peaks as well as going compass north. When they reached a habitat approximating their point of origin, they rooted, and in many cases, thrived.

For these flora, disjoined on the high heaths and crags, the choice was to reconcile with the new environment or perish. From the large numbers of species now found to occupy only Grandfather Mountain and a few other regional peaks, either as the northern or southern limits of their range, we know that many of them made it.

To duplicate all the habitats of these select southern Appalachian highlands at a sea level locale would require a three-day drive from Georgia to Newfoundland, the route that many species took when they relocated in Western North Carolina.

On Grandfather this equivalent range of native environments can be reached in a single three hour hike. Near the summit at 5,800 feet, the forest will be 98% different than 3,000 feet below. Let us pause here at the high ridgetop to view what we do understand about the workings of this rare highland world.

The science of ecology studies the interaction of organisms within their environment. On a grand scale, this weave of relations creates ecosystems, the interplay of whole communities of organisms, like a Great Barrier Reef or Everglades or Southern Appalachians. This Olympian arena nurtures numerous distinct communities, i.e. the combined populations of flora and fauna within a specific natural area. A prominent such community on the Grandfather would be the spruce-fir forests that dot (and previously wrapped all around) the shoulders of the mountain within a thousand feet of the summit.

Such communities in turn incorporate habitats, the natural environment of a single organism or species, for example a stand of mixed live and dead Fraser Fir edging a north slope boulderfield, the particular nesting and hunting grounds for the Northern Flying Squirrel. Habitats thus exist within communities, communities within ecosystems.

Grandfather Mountain is best regarded as an ecosystem of its own, hosting numerous diverse communities and habitats. These defined areas are intact, but not necessarily circumscribed or drawn absolutely in the mountain's granite; they interrelate and blend with others, evolve, change and sometimes die as species do. We can easily define the transition from spruce-fir community to an adjacent northern hardwoods forest, but lower down the emergence from classic southern hardwood forest to an Acidic Cove environ will escape the notice of all but the most expert.

Given that natural communities, in the words of the North Carolina Natural Heritage Program report which studied Grandfather Mountain, "tend to vary continuously in complex patterns across the landscape", the classifications of community types themselves may be viewed as changeable and impermanent. Indeed, they are currently labeled not as types but as 'approximations', an honest assessment of a very young scientific method only beginning to understand the interplay of so many forces at work.

In all the Appalachians, only nearby Roan Mountain exhibits a diversity and integrity of habitats approaching that of Grandfather Mountain. These two peaks model the new research modes for understanding ecology and measuring ecological health in the region.

As we survey from the summit, Grandfather's rocky ridge spine more closely resembles western American massifs rising bare above the treeline. Here, at elevations above 5,500 feet, Grandfather's crags and cliffs only appear barren.

This sub-alpine environment actually supports thriving, if very rare and fragile, natural communities. The North Carolina Heritage program report calls them *High Elevation Rocky Summit* and *Montane Acid Cliff* approximations. These ridgetop areas, as anyone standing on them will attest, are fully exposed to the prevailing elements. Soil is consequently shallow and poor, except for deep wind-blown accumulation in the crevices and niches among the stones.

Scientists discovered that the earliest Grandfather Window formations and the later Cambrian rock had vastly different acidic content, creating the basis for different flora to flourish. Due to the jumbled figuration of overhangs and recesses, the amounts of sun, wind, and rain reaching into these semi-protected habitats varied widely as well.

It is no wonder then that so many Canadian and sub-arctic plant species found their niche here as life returned northward after the ice. Grandfather Mountain has the largest, best developed, and most diverse examples of these relict communities in the Appalachians. Many threatened and endangered species grow here, some so rare they are found only on Grandfather and a few other peaks, notably Roan Mountain, standing over 6,000 feet southwest in the Unicoi Mountains on the North Carolina - Tennessee border.

Nestled in the rocks or hugging the thin topsoil, Grandfather's high elevation species include Michaux's Saxifrage, Alleghany Sand Myrtle, Wretched Sedge, Blue Ridge Goldenrod, Heller's Blazing Star, Mountain Bluet, and Rock Gnome Lichen. By now well adapted to their adopted home, these plants are vulnerable mainly to atmospheric degradations like acid rain, and, in their small remote colonies, thoughtless climbers and trailbreakers. Lichen especially, with their tenuous, indeed rootless, hold on exposed rock and trunk, are prey to the careless hand or foot.

Careful attention should indeed be paid to this oft overlooked, yet remarkable organism. Lichen are a symbiosis of a fungus and an alga that reproduce simultaneously. Together they produce their own food, survive without moisture for months, break down solid rock, and live anywhere, from the arctic to the tropics. They are a critical winter food source for flying squirrels and many other animals, and both enrich and stabilize the soil base. Litmus and other dyes are still obtained from them. Some scholars believe that a desert variety of wind-blown lichen was the biblical manna from heaven.

Other hardy flora that thrive at the upper elevations include grassy sedges, mosses, and moss-like liverworts, primitive non-flowering plants that grew over much of the earth for millions of years before pollen producing flowers evolved. Like lichen, the mosses and liverworts, or *Bryophyta*, live just about anywhere except in the sea. There are over four hundred species of these moisture loving plants in the southern mountains, almost a third of the total number, and the highest concentration in North America.

One naturalist found a key to their survival in his desk. Wetting a dry moss sample he found in a laboratory drawer, he was astonished to watch it begin to grow again. Further research proved that it had lain there unattended for fifteen years.

Mosses were the first green land plants to develop in the process of evolution. They never changed much beyond their present make-up, perhaps because their ancient form performed their functions so well. They are a valuable food source, but perhaps most importantly provide the first link in the soil formation and filling in of barren habitat, a kind of pioneer species.

Latched on to the mineral laden rock at Grandfather's summit, lichen and moss lay the groundwork for the rich colonization that followed. One species, the Grandfather Mountain Leptodontium, is both endemic and confined exclusively to the mountain, earning it the Nature Conservancy's highest rare and endangered G1 rating; 'critically and globally imperiled'.

Though the numbers of plants and flowering herbs that subsequently took root in the thin but stable soil of the summit areas were not great, their variety was. We cannot accord them all a close look, but as we descend from Calloway's Peak, keeping closely to the trail, we come to the Attic Window, where we will find one of the most delicate and beautiful.

Under the window (the appropriate name for perhaps the highest outcrop of the view to the venerable core) spreads a large colony of the rare Alleghany sand-myrtle. With its evergreen leaves, cluster of white blossoms, and red stamens, this Appalachian relict very closely resembles the Alpine azalea of New Hampshire's White Mountains.

As with many of the disjunct species, the Alleghany sand-myrtle poses a continuing problem for botanists; is it the same species as its northern forebear, different entirely, or a sub-species? In long adaptation to specific conditions on Grandfather, the myrtle is unquestionably not identical to the azalea, but are the changes varietal or substantial?

These are not mere academic exercises: plant classification tied to rarity and protection can involve extensive research, large grant funding, trail modification or closing, and even the possibility of land-use regulations under local or state law or the Endangered Species Act.

A prime example is the Bent Avens, a beautiful flowering herb and one of the rarest plant species in the world, surviving only on Roan and Grandfather Mountains. But are the relict colonies here the northern arboreal Bent Avens, or a typically southern mountain mimic or subspecies? The precise nature of the avens will determine its status of protection, and may further complicate efforts by scientists, officials, and landowners seeking to coordinate its protection.

Naturalist Harlan Kelsey, who made Grandfather Mountain his life's devotion, cites two other examples. Varieties of Hobblebush Viburnum, a northern woodland species, and the Yellow Beadlily, a Canadian tundra dweller, both inhabit the mountain's upper reaches. And most disjunct of all, wedged in rock and cliff crevices alongside Mountain Bluet and Dwarf Dandelion, lives the dusty-grey Alleghany Nailwort, bearing a striking resemblance to the famed Edelweiss of the Swiss Alps. Finally, the Turkeybeard Beargrass, a species common above 5,500 feet on Grandfather, is also common in a variety of other habitats, including a locale as different as the Pine Barrens of southern New Jersey.

The large number of mimics on the mountain, and throughout the region, have led to speculation that the Blue Ridge were at one time connected to other mountain chains. One theory holds, citing both geological and botanical evidence, that a contiguous range of mountains once uplifted from the Scottish Highlands through eastern America down the Andes to the southern tip of the South American continent. It is more likely, though by no means certain, that, as in human development, these similarities grew from parallel development under like conditions.

The thin soils of the exposed cliff and crag communities are also the basis for the hardy inhabitants of the high elevation Heath Balds of Grandfather and other peaks above 5,500 feet. The Southern Appalachian balds, another rare and endemic habitat, have been studied extensively by scientists for decades, but remain a mystery. They are upland meadows, virtually treeless, but brimming with an abundance of flora, especially the forest succession *Ericaceae,* or heath shrubs. These heath species include many of the most loved and recognized flowering plants of the region; the varieties of Rhododendron, Mountain Laurel, Blueberry, Huckleberry, and Flame Azalea.

Succession shrubs flourish after dramatic deforestation, usually some combination of clear-cutting, fire, flood, or grazing. They are therefore common throughout the Appalachians. The heath balds, however, show no uniform signs of either fire or other human intrusion. Neither do they offer any proof of original forestation or a reason why they should have developed as grassy meadows in a terrain of otherwise dense woodland.

Explanations of these open oases range from ice to blight damage to tree clearing by the Cherokee or Woodland peoples, but they could realistically comprise any of a number of combinations of human and natural events. The dense thickets of heath shrubs that vie for dominance with the grassy sedges leave little room among them for flowering herbs, and often it is only the perennial galax that can survive under their mantle.

Neither galax nor the heath *Ericaceae* restrict themselves to the balds, but will grow anywhere that canopy breaks allow in enough sunlight. It is on the open upper reaches of the mountain, however, where they bloom in most stunning profusion.

The finest examples of heath bald communities in the Appalachians undoubtedly reside on Roan Mountain and at Craggy Gardens along the Blue Ridge Parkway, but spectacular growth also occurs on Grandfather, especially on the sun-drenched south slope, easily accessible from the Parkway.

Just below the Grandfather's summit communities, we enter the sweep of upland forest. At the highest elevations, the Red spruce and Fraser fir forest etch their green-black strokes against the ridgeline, then march down the slopes almost 1,000 feet. These evergreens actually crown the summits of many of the more eroded nearby peaks, including Mount Mitchell, the highest mountain east of the Mississippi, at almost 6,900 feet. The North Carolina Blue Ridge represents the southernmost extent of the range for this Canadian boreal forest, whose ancestral home is the frozen tundra of Quebec.

The southern Spruce-Fir ecosystem, like the other Canadian relict communities, has evolved on Grandfather and other regional peaks into a woodland distinct from its forerunner.

A number of both deciduous and evergreen secondary tree species thrive under the umbrella of these two dominant conifers, including Yellow Birch, Canadian Hemlock, earliest spring blooming Serviceberry, Mountain Ash and Mountain Maple. Dense thickets of succession blackberry grow in the open understory, sometimes choking out the delicate herb species. Where the canopy has been allowed to spread, shieldferns, sedges, and mosses grow abundantly in the peatlike soil. Bluet, Wood-Sorrel, Blue Beadlily and Canada Mayflower will decorate the moss carpet in these open places.

At around 5,000 feet, we notice the dark evergreens thinning, and we can see one of the clearest community transitions of the high Appalachian ecosystem; from the Spruce-Fir to the classic Northern Hardwood Forest. This Northern Hardwood system occasionally adjoins and mingles in transition with the balsams and spruce up to about 6,000 feet, but dominates the slopes directly below their elevation limits.

Here again the high Smokies and Blue Ridge represent the southernmost extension for this non-endemic forest community. The hardwoods form a band on Grandfather Mountain between the mid-slope coves and the evergreens, although often subtly merging into both. The healthy canopy here will be a mixture of Yellow Birch, Yellow Buckeye, Beech, Black Cherry and the odd Red Spruce, Carolina and Eastern Hemlock, and White Pine. This highest elevation mixed mesophytic (moisture loving) deciduous forest can be commonly found throughout the region, but look on Grandfather for the rare abundance of the Black Cherry.

Once prominent throughout the eastern half of the country, the Black Cherry suffered from being one of the most prized cabinet woods in North America. Along with the Sugar Maple and Black Walnut, it was cut extensively for its beautifully figured wood even before the all-out logging of the 19th century. The remaining cherry trees on Grandfather's slopes are mature second or succession growth -- most of the virgin trees are gone -- but perhaps because of the difficult terrain, these forests were not cut over a second and third time; they remain some of the finest examples left outside Smoky Mountain National Park.

Heath species, especially blackberry, grew back in the sun-drenched aftermath of the massive timber cutting. Less distressed sections of these woods, probably those steeper slopes where the trees could only be selectively cut, feature the greater diversity and flowering beauty attendant on natural woodland cycles: Highbush Blueberry, Mountain Ash, Fire Cherry, Witch Hobble, Mountain Cranberry and Catawba Rhododendron.

Many of the flowering herbs found in the Northern Hardwood Forest, when not choked out by the quick succession shrubs, are identical to those in the adjacent balsams above, but are most plentiful in what are termed the *Acidic Cove* and *Rich Cove* forests of the mid-level slopes.

Acidic coves are a very nebulous transition zone, probably best distinguished by frequent, and often huge, stands of rhododendron, between the hardwood and the true cove forests lower down the slopes. The canopy may closely resembles both neighbor communities, but neither wildflowers nor flowering sub-canopy trees can flourish in the often impenetrable thickets (or hells as they are called, well understood by anyone caught in them).

You won't need a guidebook in your hand when you descend into the Rich Cove Forest. The slope will graduate and level out into a bowl, or cove. You will hear water, not the rushing of higher creekheads and wellsprings, but the burble and trickle of the branch as it spreads through the thick carpet of the understory, depositing nutrient silt in an arterial fan.

If this were the southwest, you would be standing in the mouth of an arroyo; in the South you would know you were deep in the delta. Behind you will tower the summits where you began the trek, to either side the flanking ridges that hold out the drying winds and arctic storms, and hold in the water.

The water spreads and the water stays. The air is redolent with soaking mosses. On a mountain of such antiquity, this stable mesic or moisture saturated environment builds up soil, minerals, and vegetation yearly and year-round. Eons of time are indeed needed; for even in this superbly regenerative arena it takes an estimated five hundred years to make just one inch of topsoil.

Prosperous indeed are the Rich Coves of the Appalachians and Grandfather Mountain. In the Great Smoky Mountains, the remaining virgin remnants of this system boast giant trees and fern floors suggesting the California redwood and Douglas fir forests of the Pacific Northwest. In the southern mountains, these natural communities represent the ultimate flowering to date of evolutionary biodiversity.

Biodiversity means the full complement of all organisms in their natural or normal patterns of abundance, a grown-up community or ecosystem.

As we rest now among the moss covered stones and logs, we no longer feel the wind at our back, but hear it whispering high overhead. Everything appears softer, the mossy stones, the hushed air, the stream trickling through filtered sunlight, the carpet of herbs, the gently rustling canopy of trees. Here in this sanctuary we can easily conjure back the American wilderness.

We have entered the mountain's temple.

Beneath the mature ceiling of Black Cherry, Yellow Birch, Silver Maple, White Ash and about thirty other species, the confines of the interior understory exude spaciousness. Here lie no thickets of blackberry or rhododendron to choke out the budding seedlings and wildflowers. Quite the reverse; in this seepy bowl grows the lushest herbage on the North American continent above the Florida sub-tropics.

The cove's basin shape serves as a catchall for more than just water. The accumulation of soil and decomposing wood and leaf -- part of the so-called biomass (all the organic matter within a given area) -- that blows and falls and runs off the mountain reaches its resting place here. It then acts as a giant mulch pile.

Rock that has tumbled off the high crags, from pebble-sized scree to twenty foot high boulders, have also settled in the year-round moisture, over the centuries leaching nutrient minerals into the ground as well as contributing to the matrix.

The larger spills actually form their own natural communities, called boulderfields. With so much exposed rock above, Grandfather Mountain's coves perfectly define the southern Appalachian boulderfield, and they are readily visible throughout the mountain's numerous watersheds. They often feature the Yellow Birch, with its propensity for germinating in rock and fallen trees. In the damp environ of the cove, the boulderfield breaks down microscopically to help grow the herb beds of ferns, flowers, mosses and grasses. Even the names of what grows here evoke the spirit of the place; Jewelweed, Shield Fern, Sweet Cicely, Waterleaf, Pink Turtlehead, Avens, Yellow Mandarin.

On the North Slope of Grandfather Mountain the Shanty Springs Branch warbles out of the ground at about 5,000 feet. In the lee of the north ridge and the Profile Rock, it rushes headlong down the mountain for about 500 feet, then slows as the incline suddenly levels. The stream spreads into a bog, strewn with stone, monolith and talus, and spongy with moss covered humus.

These few acres may be the finest example of a Rich Cove community in the Blue Ridge Mountains, supporting the highest concentration of plant diversity on Grandfather, and one of the richest natural herb gardens in the entire Appalachians. This exceptional place is called The Glade.

Look here for dazzling spring displays of the most beloved mountain flowers; the lilies and (Lily family) trilliums. As early as March, Purple Trillium spread their bloom among the Spring beauties. The profusion spreads to include Trout Lily, Yellow Broadlily, White Trillium, Painted Trillium, Dogtooth Lily, and the Carolina Lily, the only fragrant member of this family in North America. The Glade contains more rare, threatened, and endangered plants than any other community on Grandfather Mountain.

The Core's Stalwart, a southern Appalachian endemic, flourishes here, one of only fifty known populations. Porter's Rockcress is likewise scattered throughout, a species known to only half a dozen sites in North Carolina.

The Glade is technically a seepy boulderfield mixed mesophytic Rich Cove forest, and includes particularly sensitive populations that have taken to the rock falls. These include the Trailing Wolfsbane, the delicate white-flowered

Appalachian Bittercress, the Pink Turtlehead (unknown outside Tennessee and North Carolina), and most important, the Bent Avens.

At the western end of the Glade's open meadow, the land starts to slope downward again toward Little Grassy Creek. Along its banks, one can look for a dandelion-like rosette of evergreen leaves framing, in the early summer, a nodding magenta flower. Look extremely carefully, in both senses of the word, for you are treading among the largest known population of one of the rarest flowering herbs on earth, so rare it merits the Nature Conservancy's highest rating for an endangered species, the G1, or 'Critically Endangered Globally'.

The North Carolina Natural Heritage Program report that pinpointed the Shanty Springs communities of the avens and other rare species was derived from relatively cursory research; no comprehensive studies have been coordinated on Grandfather Mountain among the many private and public agencies that recognize its importance. In this light the report rightly concludes that there is a "high potential" for further discoveries of rare and endangered flora all over the mountain, but especially on the North Slope and in coves like the Glade.

Mindfully now, as you gravitate out of the Glade, head down the mountain again into the mixed woodlands that characterize the lower slopes. Common below 4,000 feet throughout the southern mountains, this forest features a dominant mix of pine; including Pitch, Virginia, Table Mountain, and Eastern White, and Oak; mainly Scarlet, White, Chestnut, Red, and Black.

The mingling of deciduous and evergreen produces a varied open canopy where Red Maple, Sassafras, and the Serviceberry can grow, and leaves the needed light openings for great blossoming thickets of the Mountain Laurel.

Grandfather's mixed forests stretch down the mountain to the Piedmont plain, and generally mirror those of the region as a whole. Although heavily logged, they are reaching maturity again in many locations, and feature many of the signature trees of the southeast; Sycamore, Hickory, Locust, Yellow Poplar, Sourwood, Flowering Dogwood and the occasional Black Walnut spared from the furniture makers' sharp eye.

The forest may look healthy, and appear to be growing toward its former splendor, but it is misleading to talk about ecosystem integrity here since the true dominant species of the eastern wilderness, the American Chestnut, was obliterated by disease throughout its range in the 1930's. Without the chestnut, this forest, though containing many other species endemic to the original, is nevertheless completely different.

A particularly extreme example of the dangers of artificially introduced organisms, probably the worst in American history, the Chestnut Blight destroyed not only trees but whole forests; not only forests, but an entire forest ecosystem. It never recovered, it is gone: the oak dominated woods that grew back are something else again.

This new mixed deciduous-evergreen forest has grown to become one of the most common and recognized in the mountain region. Look for dogwood predominant in the understory, except where the still threatening dogwood anthracnose virus has taken its toll; primarily in heavily shaded areas. (This threat to southern woodlands also represents a systemic breakdown, as the anthracnose was a recognized and minor issue for dogwoods prior to the mid-1980's. Suddenly, and still mysteriously they lost their immunity to the disease.) Here also are the vine Virginia creeper, the common herb Goldenrod, and Galax.

This flowering perennial is perhaps less beloved for its spiky white May bloom than the burnished beauty of its coppery evergreen leaves that light up otherwise drab brown slopes in winter. Picked for their color in wreaths and other decorative displays, galax remains common throughout the southern Appalachians, including Grandfather, up to 5,000 feet, preferring the drier southern and eastern inclines.

As Michaux noted, however, the distinguishing feature of the Blue Ridge Mountain forests, Grandfather preeminent among them, is ever-present water. Even on his wind and sun swept south slope, characteristically the driest and least diverse on most other southern mountains, tumbling waters carve greenways to the sea. The reason is that Grandfather's long summit ridgeline stands astride the Eastern Divide, the crest of the Blue Ridge that separates the Mississippi-Gulf of Mexico efflux from waters that flow into the Atlantic Ocean.

Grandfather consequently drains into five river systems. Some source books claim it is the only mountain where rivers or their feeder streams run off in all four compass directions; the North Fork of the New River flows north to the Ohio, the Watauga and North Toe run west to the Tennessee, the Linville flows south to the Catawba, and the Yadkin and Catawba, fed by Wilson's Creek, stream east to the Atlantic.

There persist repeated, if unsubstantiated, claims for the New River as the second oldest on earth, sparking a still unresolved debate awaiting conclusive data and dating methods for waterways of such antiquity. However old, Grandfather's rivers reflect the longevity and stability of his other natural components. Steady rains keep the flows constant, and the eons' accumulation of biomass along the banks and borders keep the rushing streams from silting even during the heaviest snowmelt or downpour. The biomass acts as both a filter and a sponge. It catches the debris, leaching out destructive excess runoff, but leaching in essential nutrients. It is a beautifully self-sustaining cycle, and has produced in Blue Ridge country what is often acknowledged as some of the purest waters on earth.

## *Fauna*

As the source of all life, aquatic habitat is, of course, particularly vital. As critical life springs and recreational resources, the waterways and watersheds are also particularly vulnerable to human interference.

Before the construction of a controversial shopping center sitting atop them, the headwaters of the Linville and Watauga Rivers on Grandfather's north side are still rated by the North Carolina Wildlife Commission as pristine quality breeding and habitat waters, two of only a very few such designations left in the mountains or the state. They are critical habitat indeed to many valuable species, none more prized by humans than the native Appalachian Brook Trout.

Western North Carolina claims over 4,500 miles of trout waters, but few now retain pure strains of this endemic species, driven to the remotest corners, and the point of extinction, by a host of man-made contrivances. Native Appalachian Brook Trout are a classic indicator species of environmental health or degradation. Trout streams must be cold, clear, and clean. They must also be free (rare these days) of introduced game species like the rainbow and brown trout stocked yearly in streams all over the mountains.

Sizeable populations of native trout continue to thrive in the highest reaches above the stocking areas, but their range is so restricted, and ever shrinking, that the Appalachian Brook Trout has been considered for classification under the Endangered Species Act.

Grandfather Mountain's remaining pristine waterways also support some of the largest populations of freshwater mussels anywhere in the country, especially the feeder streams to the extraordinarily mussel-rich Tennessee River. New state sponsored initiatives to save critical aquatic habitat hinge on these benchmark bivalves who give the first indications of degradation, be it rising acidity, temperature, siltation, or toxification.

The Watauga River, whose once immaculate source waters -- now fallen prey both at the head and downstream to resort development -- were considered one of the prime control areas for this and other aquatic research in the mountains. With a new shopping center (a much larger and even more destructive effort was stopped by public outcry and state agencies investigating siltation of the river) sitting directly on top of the headwaters, the future of the Watauga as a pristine stream and designated trout breeding water must now be held seriously in doubt.

If the freshwater mussel and native Brook Trout have garnered recent attention for Grandfather's waterways, another aquatic animal, the salamander, has brought him international acclaim for over one hundred years. The southern Appalachians are, in one naturalist's words, "herpetological holy ground". By that same token, Grandfather is their innermost shrine.

On this mountain of superlatives, even such would-be hyperbole is scientific fact; Grandfather is home to salamanders that are in a class by themselves: or family, rather, the family *Plethodontidae.* The plethodons, or lungless salamanders, are the only vertebrate species known to have originated in the southern Appalachians, and the evidence of numbers of species and numbers of members of species signifies Grandfather as the historical point source.

Salamanders are extremely variable in marking and coloration, so experts continue to debate the exact number of North American species, with estimates as high as 79 overall. Regional figures are more conclusive; there are 38 varieties in the Smokies and Blue Ridge, and an astonishing twenty-one confirmed species on Grandfather Mountain alone.

Three of these species, the Weller, Yohnalossee, and Northern shovel-nosed salamander, were first discovered and are thought to be endemic to the mountain. No other single location on earth affords either such diversity or concentration of these secretive, yet often spectacular creatures.

Plethodons are remarkable because they have neither gills nor lungs; they breathe through their skin and the roof of the mouth. To absorb oxygen their skin must always remain moist. They thereby particularly avoid direct sunlight, spending most daylight hours under stones in streams and bywaters, then becoming active at dusk for foraging.

Perhaps because of their retiring and nocturnal nature, or due maybe to some residue of the human distaste for reptiles as slimy and vicious (the great naturalist Linnaeus described them in terms of utter loathing and horror), salamanders attract little public attention.

To correct this injustice, take a flashlight up on one of Grandfather's trails as dusk fades on a spring evening, or lift up stones like a child at the edge of a bog or branch. Soon you will see them. You can spot the smallest American salamander here, the Pigmy, just an inch or two long - or unveil the fantastical (and harmless) hellbender; three pounds heavy and two and a half feet long, the second largest in the world.

Look also for the bright red throat patch of the Appalachian Woodland, the blue and black mottling of the Marbled, or the striking yellow and orange polka dots of the Spotted Salamander. Hybrids and the above-mentioned coloration changes from individual to individual make species identification challenging and fun.

Despite the general population's lack of interest, biologists and knowledgeable amateur naturalists have been coming to study Grandfather's salamanders for years. Dr. Emmet R. Dunn, an esteemed early twentieth century herpetologist regarded as the patron saint of the family *Plethontidae,* often collected on the mountain.

Nightwalking the old Yonahlossee Road that traversed the lower south slope, Dunn glimpsed a big specimen in his torch light. It was large and boldly marked; showing white below a chestnut red backstripe. Even before the successful capture, the expert Dunn knew he had found an entirely new species. In an unusually modest gesture after such an important discovery, Dunn named it not after himself but dubbed it the Yonahlossee Salamander. This vicinity, now Highway 221 where it meets the Blue Ridge Parkway, is still fine salamander locale.

Another Grandfather native Plethodon engendered one of the most remarkable discoveries ever made in North American herpetology. Worth Hamilton Weller was born in Cincinnati, Ohio on May 28, 1913. By his early teens he had already shown a propensity and aptitude for the reptilians, and established an impressive record of observations for the Ohio Natural History Museum. At age sixteen he became a member of the Junior Society of Natural Sciences, a year later joining the Cincinnati Society of Natural History. That same year, as a junior in high school, he scheduled his first serious research trip during his summer vacation. He naturally decided to go to the source: Grandfather Mountain.

He failed to record his first impressions as he looked up the north slope of the mountain preparing for his first climb: perhaps he had been shocked speechless. The great rolling floor of mountain forest he so eagerly anticipated had been utterly destroyed. The plague of clear-cutting had come to Grandfather

Mountain in those Depression years, followed by the pestilence of fire and flood: Weller's wild reptile vision surveyed a lifeless mudslide scarred with burned stumps.

Looking to the summit, he could see a few stands of spruce and fir among the high crags that had survived the devastation, and he decided to climb. Whether as excited teenager or dispassionate scientist, Weller likewise never printed his feelings when he reached the spot, turned over a few logs, and immediately unearthed a number of gold-spotted salamanders never before recorded in history. At the age of seventeen, he had walked through fire and discovered his own new species.

Perhaps as he trudged up the char he remembered the meaning for the word salamander, predating by centuries their scientific classification as a group of reptiles. From the Greek salamandra; a mythological reptile resembling the lizard, reputed to be able to endure or live in fire. And from the Middle Ages, the Swiss alchemist Philippus Paracelcus coined a theory of elemental substances, including one *Salamandre*, the Spirit Who Lived in Flames.

The specimens that Weller brought home to Cincinnati confirmed his taxonomy of a new species, and *Plethodon welleri* was formally introduced to the world. As a senior he graduated with honors, and planned a return trip to Grandfather that summer to collect additional data and specimens for the museum.

One week later Weller and a companion had uncovered a total of 35 more plethodons in the same area of the north slope. Descending the steep scarp after another good day's catch, Worthington Weller fell off the rocks and died instantly. He had possibly been just one step away from joining the pantheon of distinguished scientists who have gravitated to Grandfather for over two and a half centuries; John Lawson, Andre Michaux, the Bartrams, John Fraser, and Asa Gray. The Weller's salamander, though endangered, survives him.

The *p. welleri* is in fact the only one of Grandfather's Plethodons to be federally listed as endangered, but new evidence gathered by none other than the Cincinnati Zoo and

Natural History Society reveal that the entire order is in serious trouble.

As with so many animals, their decline can be traced to hunting and habitat loss. Salamanders are trapped to be used as live bait for catching bass, an activity innocently pursued with little idea of a mortal threat to entire species. Deadlier, and more unthinking still, is the destruction of the woods and waterways that sustain them.

The Cincinnati scientists estimate that four *million* salamanders have been killed this decade in North Carolina alone, primarily through rapid development and destruction of habitat in the mountains. It is no exaggeration to state that the survival of this entire host of creatures may depend on the careful preservation of their habitat on Grandfather Mountain. Although reptiles are not generally regarded as a prime feature of the Appalachian region, the southern highlands also maintain a fair representation; seven species of lizard, mainly skinks, fifteen turtles, and twenty-six varieties of snakes.

The federally endangered bog turtle, easily identified by the bright orange or red patch on the side of its head, can be found in moist areas of the Julian Price and Moses Cone Parks along the Blue Ridge Parkway. This beautiful area, fed by the Linville River and representing the northeast reach of Grandfather's slopes, is something of an ecological anomaly.

The parks are essentially man-made; the creation, and gifts to the public, of two of North Carolinas wealthiest magnates and philanthropists of the same name. Damming the river and carving out open parkland, the two estates offer unusually protected habitat for such upland elevations. They are consequently abundant in wildlife, especially aquatic species of birds, mammals, and reptiles.

As in the region generally, only two of the myriad snake species found on Grandfather are poisonous; the copperhead and the eastern timber rattlesnake. Unlike many of their southwestern and wetland counterparts, these two mountain pit vipers are both shy, retiring, and rarely confront, much less bite, the casual visitor.

Much more commonly found are the rat, garter, king, and water snakes, easily recognized as the denizens of creeks and backyards throughout the eastern United States. One may be fortunate enough to encounter a hog-nosed snake, a harmless and particularly gentle species that makes up for its lack of real aggression by turning on a ferocious display of puffing, hissing, spreading, and coiling when disturbed. If all else fails and the intruder stands its ground, the hog-nosed will roll over and play dead.

This behavior is an apt metaphor for the relationship, and the outcome of the relationship, between human and reptile. To consider the pervasive view of these creatures, simply turn to your thesaurus. It lists three synonyms for 'reptiles': 'Animal', followed by 'Groveler', then 'Scoundrel'. Now look further under 'Animal' and read 'Creature', or 'Savage'. If the reptiles continue to suffer from our prejudice and general indifference, they can stand to benefit from the avoidance this ignorance entails, hiding from the fearful and violent reaction to an image that has been conjured up in so many peoples' minds. At least they are considered useless.

Not so our closest cousins, the mammals. From the very earliest moments in our prehistory we have actively pursued them; for food, fur, and horn, companionship, sport and display. Many species today are more likely found hanging on walls and hanging on in the wild by the thinnest of margins; many have vanished altogether.

Nevertheless, a great diversity of warm-blooded life continues to survive in the United States, in the Southern Appalachians, and on Grandfather Mountain. Mammals began their run for global dominance in the Mesozoic era more than 170 million years ago. The herds and predators that roamed most of the earth's surface were often fierce and enormous, great ungulate, feline, equine, and elephantine beasts featuring huge tusks, teeth and antlers. They roamed deserts, jungles, ice packs, and mountains. It is, at least in part, testament to our own ferocity that the then emerging human race successfully competed with, and ultimately conquered them in order to survive.

The igneous-based southern mountains have neither the glacial activity nor the soft sedimentary rock necessary to imprint and preserve true fossil remnants of the Pleistocene. With few sediments and no rock from this period Grandfather region shows no evidence of this era. Unlike the desert southwest or frozen arctic, there are no perfect fern outlines on soft rock or complete mammoth skeletons exposed by thaw.

While not one such exact reproduction has been found here, migratory patterns of the early mammal herds traversing the southern mountains are indeed traceable. The evidence is botanical, with preserved seeds and soil content showing that even millions of years ago, these temperate highlands offered fine habitat for both northern and southern species.

From the boreal forests came saber-tooth tiger, wooly mammoth, mastodon, and forest ox. They would have had to compete with jaguar, peccary, tapir, giant ground sloth, spectacled bear and other indigenes known to have spread up from the Central American sub-tropics.

Many of the species have of course died out, and many have evolved, but some, like the bear, seem to have survived unchecked and unchanged downs the millennia. The spectacled bear, or tremarctos, remains today the only South American bear. It inhabits upland forests, is wide-ranging and omnivorous and usually exhibits some (highly variable) white facial markings. In all but this one cosmetic regard, he is indistinguishable from our common American black bear.

The black bear can itself show colors ranging from blue-black to chocolate brown to cinnamon brown to white, and sometimes exhibit the different phases within the same litter. Some scientists consider then that the two animals, spectacled and black, are one and the same, and that the spectacled bear may be the forerunner of the other.

Intriguing as this exotic mammalian melange must have been, it was also literally doomed; the climatic fluctuations of the ice ages would have played hell with all that highly specialized equipment; great size, teeth, shaggy coats, etc. Unable to adapt, they were consigned to the dustbin of evolution.

All except for the bear. The ursus' combination of congruous temperament and skills have insured them, then and now, a successful role in most of the earth's environments. They eat just about everything, and will travel up to fifteen square miles a day to do so. They can run, fight, climb, dig, and swim in equal measure, then reduce their vital signs to near-comatose levels to sleep it all off.

The southern Appalachians have one of the largest black bear populations in the country, but with their mobility and inclination to wander, the exact numbers are very hard to gauge. Three sightings on Grandfather in a 24-hour period could be three animals, or the same one. The numbers are important, and bitterly contested, in determinations of what makes a healthy sustainable population, whether they are increasing or declining, and how well the bear is being 'managed' on public lands. With its combination of protected federal and sparsely populated privately owned property, Grandfather offers critical sanctuary to this species that exists increasingly under the cloud of diminished room to live.

As most of the bear's prehistoric co-habiters died out, many new species developed to fill the abhorred vacuum, more streamlined, intelligent, and adaptable. By the time the first human predators, clutching their spear throwers, padded watchfully up the Watauga, the New, and the Linville Rivers, they were tracking a great host of creatures: bison, elk, moose, caribou, mountain lion, black bear, white-tailed deer, bobcat, red and grey wolf, red and grey fox, beaver, mink, river otter, long-tailed and least weasel, fisher, spotted and striped skunk, fox, red, northern and southern flying squirrel, mink, woodchuck, muskrat, possum, raccoon, bog lemming, hare, and rabbit.

Many of their tracks and traces, especially of the larger animals, have long since vanished from Grandfather Mountain, but a majority survive, and knowingly or not, we walk among them as our ancestors did. They are fewer to be sure, and more elusive for good   reasons. Although many mammals are nocturnal, and wary by nature, our deadly hunting skills, and later sheer numbers, have driven them increasingly to ground.

The most significant case in point concerns the mountain lion.

The mountain lion, or cougar, puma, panther, or catamount, is the largest, shyest, and most endangered of the seven North American wild cats, which include the lynx and the only other Appalachian resident feline, the bobcat.

In Peter Matthiessen's words:

> The fierce bobcat, prolific and resourceful, has matched the success of the coyote in its efforts to circumvent man and remains widely distributed, though not plentiful. But the cougar, ... which once prowled every state in the nation, and, ranging south to the Argentine, had the most extensive range of all North American mammals, is a species in full retreat. In early times the cougar was confused extensively with the African lion (until the chronic absence of a lion with a mane encouraged a reappraisal) a fact which may have led to the observation, in 1800, that 'it is fierce and ravenous in the extreme...'
>
> Actually, it is the most timid of the world's large cats, and as in the case of the North American gray wolf, despite the wild-eyed tales in today's outdoor magazines, the documented instances of cougar attacks on human beings, in all the history of North America, can be counted on the fingers of one hand. Nevertheless, it is a skilled killer of game, and more rarely, of domestic animals, and as such was outlawed. Solitary, and never numerous enough to warrant the campaigns which banished the wolf, it is nonetheless destroyed wherever found and is hunted commonly in the name of sport.

Sightings had been thought so rare in the Blue Ridge and Smoky Mountains that this foremost predator of an entire continent has been listed by all official agencies as officially extirpated and extinct in its Appalachian range.

Except that it *isn't*, and sightings there indeed are. Within the last five years alone, two horses attacked in Crossnore, North Carolina, less than ten miles from Grandfather, bore feline claw marks much too large for a bobcat. A mother with cub was seen silhouetted along a ridge in Penland, and a long black-tipped tail spotted crossing the Blue Ridge Parkway late at night, at the foot of Grandfather Mountain.

There have been additional (and numerous) sightings by those who patrol the federal holdings between dusk and dawn; the park rangers, foresters, and other employees who must then report them, or often not, to agencies which categorically refute that possibility. The official line stipulates that these cougars, if they *are* cougars, are escapees from game parks and private homes and collections. Unfortunately for this explanation, the sightings are documented, but the disappearances from these zoos and owners are not. Shortages of both funds and bureaucratic motivation have left the question of Appalachian mountain lions unresolved, and largely unstudied.

One study from Lees-McRae College in Banner Elk, North Carolina, involved an 'anecdotal' survey that included respondents from all over the North Carolina and adjacent Tennessee mountain region. The survey resulted in so many accurate reports of cougars in the area, that the study concluded that the question is not whether the cougar exists in the Appalachians, but *how many* exist, as well as many other questions regarding their biology.

The questions regarding their exact genetic makeup, i.e. are these western or Florida or inbred or altered species of cougar, are moot for the moment in the face of the overwhelming need to save them whatever and wherever they are.

The method commonly employed to rescue a population in its final throes, now in effect, (and embroiled in controversy), to save the Florida panther, California condor, and others, is called captive breeding. The entire wild population, usually declined to a few dozen individuals trapped in a restricted area, is captured. They are bred in captivity, then a few breeding pairs slowly released in a controlled environment like an island. Once self-sufficiency has been re-attained, whatever numbers deemed necessary for successful wild breeding are released in the wild: other pairs continue to produce stock for additional release.

One of the most established and successful -- by some standards -- current ventures of this kind is a North Carolina-based U.S. Fish and Wildlife Service project to reintroduce the Red Wolf to its original range throughout the southeast, including the Smoky and Blue Ridge Mountains.

The Red Wolf is smaller, shyer, and grouped in families rather than the packs of its notorious gray cousin, but it nevertheless caught much of the firestorm rained down upon the Gray wolf. It was likewise hunted almost to extinction, and driven to breeding with coyotes to survive.

Their capture, select breeding (on a remote island off the Carolina coast) and carefully monitored release in a number of wilderness areas, represents the only successful reintroduction to date of a carnivorous mammal in North America. The wolves are reportedly surviving, and breeding, in wild areas of eastern North Carolina, but have not fared so well in the Smoky Mountains, where harsher natural conditions have made their lives more difficult. A legal challenge by hunters and citizens adjacent to some of the release locations to kill the wolves if they strayed from the protected areas was recently defeated in court, and more releases are planned.

Another major reintroduction into the Smokies, that of the North American elk, is being held up by state officials who fear the spread of something similar to Europe's dreaded Mad Cow Disease, although supporters can point to successful new herds in states throughout the country, with no incidence of the disease. In Western North Carolina, a successful effort in the Smokies would likely be followed by smaller reintroductions on game lands, including areas near Roan Mountain and Grandfather.

For the moment, all the elk and native wolves, gray and red, have gone from Grandfather Mountain.

The outlook for the mountain lion remains very bleak.

River otters, hunted and driven out from the mountains by the 1960's, have been reintroduced to the Catawba River, fed by Wilson's Creek and tributaries along Grandfather's south slope. Their comeback will depend on maintaining water quality and large areas of pristine, undisturbed aquatic habitat. No accurate assessment of the populations of the many smaller mammals surviving on and around the mountain exists.

One of Grandfather's most esteemed inhabitants, the northern flying squirrel, is also one of the most endangered throughout this southernmost portion of its range. Midway in size between the fox and red squirrels, the respectively largest and smallest U.S. tree squirrels, the flyers are carnivorous and nocturnal. They nest in large colonies, often twenty at a time, in dead tree cavities hollowed out by woodpeckers. They prefer mature conifers and hardwoods, and will appear in broad daylight only if disturbed, decamping in a startling flurry of flapping fur. The squirrels steer with their tails and can glide, and indeed flap, up to several hundred feet in one flight. Their habitat range is up to seventy acres.

The Grandfather Mountain population is rated by the North Carolina Natural Heritage Foundation survey as "incredibly significant". Not only endangered but declining and isolated, this population of undetermined numbers is living at the very southern tip of its range, in competition with other, more aggressive species, and faced with destruction of their nesting areas and their primary food sources, moss and lichen. Attempts to coax some individuals into special nesting boxes around the Glade, and to determine their existing nests on Grandfather Mountain, have to date been unsuccessful.

Grandfather's waterways support mink, muskrat (look for four to six-foot openings in the mud streambanks), possibly fisher, beaver (at Cone and Price Parks), and the least and long-tailed weasel. The least weasel is no larger than a chipmunk, the smallest carnivorous mammal in North America, but one of the most ferocious. Again, the weasel is a northern boreal species living at the southern end of its range; its precise numbers and condition on Grandfather Mountain remain unknown.

Gray and red fox coexist on the mountain as elsewhere, the gray staking out the deep woods, and the red nesting and hunting in brush, meadow, and other open areas. Singled out for centuries as a prized sport and pelt target, the fox continues to survive by its peerless wits and wiles.

No one will (or should!) have any difficulty spotting the familiar eastern striped skunk, or polecat, but one might be surprised to happen on its rarer and more retiring cousin, the spotted skunk, about half the size and sometimes referred to in these parts as a civet cat. These non-aggressive creatures will not spray you unless startled or badgered.

We must not overlook the diminutive pygmy shrew, barely two inches long and weighing only as much as a dime. It is the smallest known living mammal on the North American continent. Five other species of shrew, four species of vole, and three species of mouse tunnel through the mountain.

As wondrous as the variety of warm-blooded life on Grandfather Mountain are their ways of life, quirky and often spectacular. Witness, for example, the Golden Mouse.

The Golden Mouse, yet another northern species realizing its southern limits on Grandfather and other regional high peaks, completely abandons the signature timidity of his brother species. Don't look down to see him, look up, *way* up. The Golden climbs and nests in trees up to thirty feet high. He furthers his visibility by his bright gold-orange fur, and if that hasn't caught your attention, by raucous chatter. On Grandfather, look for him in large hemlocks standing in damp boulderfields.

You may happen upon a New England cottontail rabbit. Watch him freeze, rather than bolt like the wary and common Eastern cottontail. Perhaps this explains why the New England steadfastly declines, and the Eastern defies all efforts at eradication.

While you are searching for other arboreal creatures, fear not for your hold on reality if you spot a skunk or fox in the leafy understory. The spotted skunk and the grey fox can both climb trees to escape from danger.

The Least Weasel exhibits a lack of adaptability every bit as curious as a fox learning to scamper up a tree trunk. This weasel inhabits aquatic forest habitats from the southern Appalachians almost to the Arctic Circle, In the northern climes, the weasel, like many other mammals and birds, will turn white in the winter. In more temperate zones it quite naturally adopts an equally well-camouflaged dark brown.

Transplant a northern weasel southward, and it will still molt to white during the cold months. And further, their Dixie counterparts will stay dark if taken to the snows of the north woods. Has a single species begun to evolve into two distinct 'races' based on latitude?

The snowshoe hare, a rare Blue Ridge visitor more often associated with the Canadian tundra and sub-Arctic, usually remains brown in its southernmost range near Grandfather

Mountain, but will molt according to the surrounding conditions. In the Arctic it will turn white with the first snows, but still in stages, so that it will be mottled in early winter in color conjunction with the patchy snows. It is also in this state that it may remain further south, where even heavy snows often melt off in mid-winter.

Many of the hare's other characteristics, however, seem better suited to the pages of *Alice in Wonderland*. It is among the smallest and shyest of all the hares, yet is a carnivore. A powerful digger, it prefers instead to nest in pre-dug woodchuck burrows. Very rare among the Lagomorphs, the snowshoe is a powerful swimmer. So, of course, it doesn't swim; like chinchillas and other desert dwellers, it takes dust baths instead, a trait not terribly well suited for damp forest.

Finally, the hare fails even to live up to its name; when threatened, it won't use all that explosive speed, but hides, not hares. When forced to break cover, it runs as madly as a march hare, continuously until exhausted, in giant circles of two acres or more, periodically jumping twelve feet in the air and hitting speeds of over 30 mph. All the fox has to do is wait.

One last exceptional resident of Grandfather Mountain merits special attention, though few people will hike up the southeastern slope for a glimpse. Here above the Linville Viaduct in the Black Rock Cliffs Cave live a colony of Virginia Big-Eared Bats, the only bat native to North Carolina.

Humans reserve some of their worst fears for the unfortunate bat, a pathological and illogical response also bestowed on sharks, wolves, snakes, and spiders. It would be enlightening to add up death and injury statistics from all these species compared to those suffered from our best friend, the family dog. There would be no comparison. Bats eat *bugs*, not people.

When the bats were first officially located on Grandfather Mountain in the mid-1980's, only about thirty individuals of this endangered species were holding on to existence in their last hideout. Normally in colonies of thousands, the best guess was that this population had declined due to intense pesticide spraying on the federal lands around the cave, fatal for a species with a voracious appetite for insects.

Under the auspices of the U.S. Fish & Wildlife Service, the cave entrance was sealed off and the spraying halted. Their recovery was nothing short of spectacular, with the population burgeoning to an estimated 10,000 individuals after just a decade of protection. And Blue Ridge Parkway visitors can now have their insect problem controlled by natural means instead of toxic chemicals.

The Virginia Big-Eared Bat is so small that over 120 have been counted sleeping in a cluster only a foot square. With ears almost half their entire body size, they fly and feed employing a radar system that, like that of dolphins, is more sophisticated than anything developed by technology.

Speaking of spiders, a recent discovery has placed Grandfather firmly in the forefront of essential arachnid inquiry. Consider this: a high-elevation eastern forest dwelling tarantula the size of a BB. This exotic creature was first discovered on Mount Mitchell in 1923, but has been disappearing from the southern highlands ever since, as their exclusive spruce-fir habitat has been decimated by introduced insect infestation and acid rain.

The Grandfather Mountain population is now the largest remaining in the world, perhaps the only viable one, a situation so grave that the Spruce-Fir Tarantula has been recommended for endangered species status by the Federal Government, only the second spider in history to be so named. Captive breeding efforts have so far failed, so if this habitat fades off Grandfather, the spider, too will probably disappear off the earth.

While few hardy souls will be found searching the upper reaches of the mountain for bats or spiders, many do come to explore one of the prime venues for birding, or birdwatching as it used to be known, in all America.

The birds of Grandfather Mountain easily rate a volume to themselves, and may one day do so. Indeed, field guides to this and just about every other region seem to proliferate like starlings. With some exceptions, this discussion will not detail the whereabouts of individual species like the Blackburnian Warbler or the Red-Breasted Nuthatch (Beacon Heights Trail, off Parkway Milepost 305.3). For inveterate birders, this sort of information is elsewhere available (see Bibliography), and here we can enjoy more of the sense and significance of Grandfather's resident avians.

First, a word on recording and identification. By all means take a field guide if you are even casually birding, but trust your ears and eyes as well. Birding is not about compiling species and life lists, but about attuning oneself to The Wild, internally as well as externally. In this spirit, be ready for anything. You can see osprey and sandpipers in the Blue Ridge Mountains. A pelican was sighted in the Smokies during a hurricane on the Carolina coast. A Buff-Bellied Hummingbird (enjoy the names, too), rarely seen north of the Rio Grande in south Texas, took up a three-day residence in a suburban Asheville, North Carolina backyard in 1989. Birds get lost too, it appears.

Avian species identification has developed into far more than just an entertaining exercise in numbers and observation. Rather, it is proving ever more critical to the survival of the many declining bird species throughout the Americas and the world. Data collected from confirmed sightings serves to tell us which species are in decline, and where, and often why. Recorded observation can pinpoint not only populations, but the relationship between the species and the ecosystem they depend upon.

Visible and popular, birds are the best indicator (of environmental deterioration) species there are; just ask the spotted owl. From Washington's Olympic Peninsula to the Platte River in the Midwest to the Everglades to the Blue Ridge, bird decline is either the first or best sign that a natural area is getting into trouble. In many cases, not just the owl's, these belated warnings have initiated successful efforts to save the remnants of both species and habitat. And all indications show that the destruction of critical habitat is, in all too many locations, reaching critical mass.

On Grandfather, studies of bird populations, both nesting and migratory, confirm the findings of ornithologists throughout the region; numbers are declining, sometimes drastically. Yet in many cases the base-numbers of breeding pairs would serve well enough for regeneration if today's greatest threats to the mountain's health, i.e. development and pollution, were not allowed to worsen further. This does not take into account what is taking place in the many migrant birds other domain, the tropical rain forests.

The most prominent case in point involves the family of tropical songbirds, the well-loved migratory warblers and other colorful passerines that winter in the southern hemisphere but breed and nest in the north, or on top of northern clime mimics like Grandfather Mountain. These magnificent songbirds grace most of the continental U.S. during their spring and fall treks of thousands of miles between their two homes.

Warblers and their cousins the tanagers, orioles, et al, probably bring out more fanatic birders than any other group of birds. Beautiful to see and hear, they can flood budding green groves or golden shedding hillsides with glorious sound and color. So when fewer and fewer return to their summer quarters or spring stopovers each year, as is now the case, alarm bells erupt in a big hurry.

Due to severe habitat destruction throughout their entire range, from South America to the Arctic, and along their entire lifeline through Central and North America, warbler populations are estimated to have dropped by *thirty percent* in just the last decade. The monumental destruction of the tropical hardwood forests has been well-documented, but it is important to understand that equal havoc is wreaked on critical habitat by 'incremental' intrusions, the proverbial death of a thousand cuts.

A clear-cut here, a housing development there, just a little bit more, and another wetland or spruce grove or berry patch is lost, and with it the foraging bear, the squirrel looking for lichen, and the warbler who may have flown 5,000 miles to return to the favored circumstances of that one area. These animals don't -- can't -- move over to the next likely spot, even if it has remained intact. That spot has already filled with its complement of species, so that those whose habitat has been destroyed will die.

Peter Matthiessen elaborates:

We are apt to think of wild animals retreating from civilization in the same way they might flee before a forest fire or flood. Actually, such retreat is ordinarily impossible, since any suitable habitat they might withdraw to is filled to capacity already by the same species. In other words, when one speaks of a species 'withdrawing' or 'retreating', one really means that it has been exterminated in certain units of its range, or that the habitats of the species within these units have been destroyed. It is the limits of the range which have retreated, for the affected animals themselves are dead.

That is why saving 'just' a few hundred acres here or there, especially on rare ground like Grandfather Mountain, takes on global ecological significance.

More than twenty species of warbler, virtually all declining, have been observed here during breeding season (April-June). Simply, the greater the variety of habitat, undisturbed habitat, the greater the variety and number of birds. Some, like the Magnolia Warbler, depend entirely on the boreal spruce and heath at the highest elevations, but in general, all portions of the mountain yield a wide selection.

The warblers' closest songbird compatriots, including grosbeaks, tanagers, Ovenbirds, Indigo Bunting, Red-Eyed and Blue-Headed (formerly Solitary) Vireos, Veery, and Wood Thrush, also distribute themselves throughout Grandfather's diverse havens. The Tanawha Trail, which traverses the south shoulder parallel to the Blue Ridge Parkway, has been rated a prime and readily accessible viewing area for many of these species, especially in late Spring and early Fall.

All told, over sixty breeding birds have been counted on Grandfather Mountain; "without doubt the most diverse assemblage of nesting birds in a small geographical area in the southeast United States", according to North Carolina State University ornithologist David Lee. To further enhance this perspective, consider that the 1984 survey that put up these numbers found 27 breeding species on Roan Mountain, and 45 in the Unicoi Mountains of Tennessee. The entire Plott Balsam Range in the central North Carolina Mountains, an area that has been studied since the 1880's, yielded 100 breeding species. Mr. Lee's month-long study concludes that "an additional 20-30 nesting species could reasonably be expected on Grandfather Mountain...the breeding fauna of Grandfather comes closer to what could normally be expected for an entire mountain chain than a single peak".

Overall, more than 150 avian species have been counted on Grandfather Mountain. This is by no means definitive; no comprehensive year to year count has ever been conducted on the mountain. Just such a review is now in the planning stages, and will undoubtedly reveal new sightings, and much valuable scientific data besides.

Many of Grandfather's birds will be familiar to anyone keeping an occasional eye on his backyard feeder. We will leave them there, and hike up the Shanty Springs Trail on a crisp April evening, a moderately strenuous affair that brings us to the shadowy Glade just before dusk.

Watch the shadows; soon one will detach and drop from the understory in an effortless glide, trajectory smooth and silent as a dream. The mouse will sense nothing until the talons strike, and nothing after. Only later, on the nest, will the owl break the quiet, trilling a few notes into the Glade.

In the dark forest that call may be the only means of knowing exactly what bird you just saw, because eight different owl species inhabit the woods and wood margins of Grandfather Mountain: the Great Horned, Eastern Screech, Long-Eared, Short-Eared, Barred, Barn, Northern Saw-Whet, and (perhaps) Snowy.

The Short-Eared (whose ears are actually almost invisible) and the majestic Snowy owl, hunting the bog lemming, would represent rare and occasional visitors from the northland. Also elusive here are the Barn and Long-Eared owls, whose status had long been doubtful in this most southern part of their range.

The 1984 survey finally recorded a breeding season sighting, or sounding rather, at the Glade, where Long-Ears were heard repeatedly over a month's time. As this owl utters a unique variety of whistles, hoots, and calls while around its nest, and is otherwise silent, this represents the first confirmed nesting site for the Long-Eared owl south of Mount Rogers in southwestern Virginia.

Great Horned owls have also been seen or heard in the Glade (larger owls frequently prey on smaller ones) as well as along the lower reaches of Wilson's Creek. They are not believed to breed on the mountain, however, which as we will see plays an important part in the life of another key avian predator, the Peregrine falcon.

The Northern Saw-Whet is the most sought after species among owl fanciers in the Blue Ridge. Shy, nocturnal, barely the size of the diminutive screech owl and lacking its tufts, The Saw-Whet is rarely seen and is identified mainly by its call, a series of short whistles. Their regional breeding area had long been thought to include Grandfather and other high-elevation peaks. They have been heard, though not known positively to nest, in the Glade, near the entrance to the Black Rock Cliffs Cave, and along the Beacon Heights Trail. Years of research finally paid off in 1995, when a nesting pair was confirmed on the mountain, though their exact location is being kept secret.

The Saw-Whet and Long-Eared owls join at least 17 other avian species, including the Ruffed Grouse, Red Crossbill, Black-capped Chickadee, Raven, and four warblers, as reaching their southern breeding limits on Grandfather, Roan, and a few other southern mountains. But ornithologists believe that an additional twenty-five species may be found to breed on the mountain once in-depth surveys can be made.

Again, from the 1984 report; "It is likely that nowhere else in North Carolina is such a rich diversity of breeding birds attained in such a restricted area as Grandfather Mountain. With even a modest amount of additional field work, well over half the state's nesting bird fauna may be documented from an area of less than ten square miles."

Two other remarkable residents of the High Country deserve special mention. Grandfather is rated on of the best locations in the Blue Ridge to view the common raven. This cliff-dwelling corvine (members of the crow family, including jays, magpies, shrikes and many Old World species) is the largest passerine or perching bird in the United States.

The raven is also regarded the most intelligent of this clever avian family. Captive birds have been taught not only to mimic, but to count, and to solve memory problems and puzzles.

Modern research has shown that mimicking goes miles beyond the common parlor trick previously assumed. It is of course the first step human parents employ to teach their language to offspring, and an ability otherwise limited to a few marine mammals, apes, and birds. Studies as early as 1971 (Chamberlin & Cornwell) report that inasmuch as communication and learning are the primary functions of language, "human language and bird song are compatible". In 1990 a California scientist examining avian brain functions and injuries made the astonishing discovery that birds, alone among all animals including human beings, can regenerate their brain cells. And with their new cells they relearn the behavior or memory or instinct that was inherent in the damaged portions of the brain.

An experiment in 1993 with a particularly gifted word-trained parrot culminated in a scene that, like the teaching of sign language to Koko the gorilla, will determine that both science and the public rethink their simplistic view of animal intelligence. Two researchers were discussing an upcoming trip to the veterinarian; scheduling and so forth, when the bird piped up from his perch, to wit: "don't take me there, I don't want to be hurt, I want to stay here".

Birds have evolved since, and perhaps from, the dinosaurs. Loons have lived on the earth for 60 million years, since approximately the time of the dinosaurs' passing. Pelicans are at least 30 million years old, ravens 12 million years.

Like many avian species, ravens mate for life. High above the Tanawha Trail's Raven Rocks, the couple's spring courtship display includes soars and glides touching wingtip to wingtip, power dives, and tumbling together in free-fall thousands of feet through the air. Ravens can flap like a crow, soar like an eagle, hover like a kestrel, circle like a buzzard. Observers have seen them, in play or deliberate challenge perhaps, hold their position absolutely motionless head-on to gale-force winds.

Ravens live from Mexican desert to Alaskan tundra to Appalachian mountain, their only U.S. residency south of Canada and east of the Rockies. They require wilderness to survive. There may be five breeding pairs on Grandfather Mountain.

The other aerial artist of Grandfather's crags and cliffs above 5,000 feet is the Peregrine falcon. Among many extraordinary attributes, the Peregrine's eyesight and wing speed stand out as the most exceptional in the bird world. On the wing, a circling falcon can spot a Mourning dove flutter on the ground a mile below. Even if the prey is completely motionless, the bird can see it from an altitude of over 3,000 feet.

From its straightaway flight, the falcon will veer off suddenly, then circle and pause, measuring the dive, or 'stoop' as falconers call it. The bird points itself downward, beginning the power plummet with a few wing beats, then drawing the wings into body and rocketing like a fired projectile. It hits its prey in mid-air at two hundred miles an hour. The dove lies broken in the hooked talons, but the peregrine has fully absorbed the shock through its massive foreclaws.

If you were watching, you only begin to breathe again as he flaps leisurely away with the kill.

Only the peregrine's close cousin, the Prairie falcon, can fly faster, up to 300 mph by some estimates, but nothing in the air can match the drama of the power dive, which is the peregrine's alone.

Although still listed as a federally endangered species, peregrines have come a long way since their near total decimation by DDT in the late 1960's. By 1970, in fact, they were thought to be almost extirpated throughout their entire range. In the summer of 1972, The Laboratory of Ornithology at Cornell University (still one of, if not the, leading avian research institutes in the world), had found a few birds and initiated a captive breeding program for peregrines at their facility in Ithaca, New York.

With their eggs protected from the shell disintegration, and the birds isolated from the toxic infection of their food chain, both results of massive pesticide spraying, they bred successfully in captivity; 20 birds in 1973, 95 in 1978, and ultimately a total of 324 healthy individuals.

Reintroduction began in 1979 at various sites around the country. The peregrines needed cliffs for nesting, and large wild areas for hunting, free from human intrusion. And they also needed areas not already staked out by another fearsome and widespread predator, the Great Horned owl, who raids their nests for both eggs and chicks.

In 1984, Grandfather Mountain's Profile Cliffs were chosen as a 'hacking' site, the first reintroduction in North Carolina and the southern Appalachians. Hacking is the site-specific nesting site reintroduction of an avian species. The previously captive birds are slowly acclimated to a suitable breeding area, fed and cared for at the site over a period of time, rather than just being thrown to the winds. One-third of all birds released in the state were done so here, a total of eleven individuals by 1989.

These efforts, in North Carolina at least, have paid off in stellar fashion. Now reintroduced throughout the mountains, at Chimney Rock Park, Pigeon River Bluffs, Hawksbill and Whitesides Mountains as well as Grandfather, the Peregrine appears to have taken well to its new old home.

With the exception of the neo-tropical migrants and a few other species, Grandfather's current bird populations appear to be relatively healthy and stable. The problem with these estimations is that they are based on the sketchiest of hard field data, and without new in-depth studies will always be more question mark than exclamation point.

As to good birding spots, there really aren't any bad ones anywhere on the mountain. No birder should leave the area, however, without a visit to Julian Price Park, especially Price Lake, Sims Creek, and Sims Pond. Here in the heart of the Blue Ridge Mountains one can find a variety of species usually associated with Canadian Lakes or South Carolina beaches; sandpiper, grebe, heron, loon, goose, teal, plover, and yellowlegs among others.

We have ranged all over the mountain, yet only just touched on Grandfather's natural diversity; a lifetime of study here would leave more secrets uncovered than revealed. But it is equally impossible, even after a brief visit, to leave empty-handed. Perhaps after all it may be the secret mountain, intact, that is the revelation.

Standing back and viewing it as a whole, it is difficult not to think ourselves back to the time when Grandfather reached its full complement of life, to imagine the spring chorus of thousands of songbirds or the shadows of elk herds moving among stands of trees five feet thick and two hundred feet high. We return to a moment of that time; the crags and coves rustling and bustling with sound and motion, when suddenly there burst upon the lower slopes a cataclysm. It is ten millennia before the present day. A thousand miles north, the last of the ice packs have receded back to the arctic, and the hosts of cliff and cove dwellers have taken their places on the mountain.

Yet the mountain has still not been completed.

When this monumental event occurred, the most explosive on Grandfather since the uproar of the Window, it resounded with the slight rustle of dead leaves, or the snap of dry twig. A doe may have bolted a clearing, or a grouse flushed as blue jays squawked their warnings. But other than these few everyday events, the mountain's inhabitants probably paid little attention to the hushed tones of that first party of hunters or gatherers as they picked their way up toward the creek head.

The humans had come.

# CHAPTER 3

## *Humans*

Imagine now everything we modern humans have left behind -- all the physical evidence from three hundred years of settlement and development on and around Grandfather Mountain. Bulldoze in your mind all the concrete and macadam, billboards and landfills and resort homes into a big pile. The resulting mountain of debris would dwarf Grandfather and every other peak in the Southern Appalachians.

But there *were* human beings living in the mountains, continually if not permanently, for over 10,000 years before the coming of the white settlers. Where is everything they made and used and threw away?

In the first place, they made little and threw away less, but that doesn't fully explain why the sum of remains from prehistoric Western North Carolina amounts to a scattering of tools and implements, barely enough for a few good yard sales. Which, sadly to say, is one of the better places to look for them.

This first fact we encounter by studying our predecessors in the Grandfather Mountain region will tell us more about us than about them. By far the majority of artifacts uncovered here have not been excavated scientifically, but picked up willy-nilly, hoarded, traded, sold off, or given away. We know so little about this part of our heritage because we have stolen it from ourselves.

Ironically, it is not lack of interest that has destroyed the bulk of archaeological record in the Blue Ridge, but exactly the opposite. Our natural fascination with the spear point found in the garden or stream bed has not been tempered by the inclination, or as in most countries, tough laws, to call the local college or historical society and have both the site and artifact examined professionally.

Objects taken out of situ, or their stratigraphic context in the ground, reveal remarkably little about their original owners. The timeline, the continuity, the development of events goes missing entirely. Trying to put together a comprehensive view of prehistoric life on Grandfather Mountain from isolated objects gathered piecemeal is like trying to make a picture with pieces from a thousand different puzzles.

What we are left with are tantalizing clues, and many, many, more questions than answers.

We do know that our first prehistoric human scouting party, members of the culture tagged the Paleo-Indians, would likely have approached the mountain following the herds and flocks of game. Most of Grandfather and the surrounding region were still covered with vast boreal forests, some mix of spruce-fir and deciduous hardwood. With its landmark shape, teeming game, nearly solid canopies blocking thick undergrowth, and plenty of waterway access, Grandfather would have been the perfect destination for cunning, mobile, and adventurous bands of hunter-gatherers.

It has always been reckoned that the earliest Americans, here as elsewhere, followed the general west to east migration pattern that began when an Asian people crossed the land-bridge, later breached, through the Bering Strait linking Siberia and North America. They then ostensibly made their way south and east across the continent.

But some recent discoveries, especially a twelve-thousand year old settlement site in Chile, thought the earliest on the continent, have led some pre-historians to believe that at least a corresponding counter movement may also have taken place from south to north, following the rush of flora and fauna from the southern hemisphere into the huge eco-gap left by the warm up of more temperate zones. In other words, at least some of the aboriginal Oriental immigrants may have kept heading south to the tropics before ever coming to eastern North America.

So the very origin of the first human beings that explored what archaeologists call the Appalachian Summit Region, and accordingly their language, bearing, social and family life, and numbers, has been called into question.

Whatever their origins, they were certainly nomadic, and the earliest evidence puts their date of arrival in Western North Carolina, probably from the west along the New River, at around 12,000 B.P. - before the present. This earliest Paleolithic period in American history lasted, at best estimate, about 4,000 years. In North America, Paleo-Indian refers inclusively to these bands -- men, women, and children -- of unsettled hunter-gatherers.

We assume their numbers were small because they left so little sign. But we can't be sure if these very few indications refer to few people, sporadic visits, or a significant human presence that may have vanished with the subsequent taking of their limited possessions.

Clovis Points have been found in the High Country and the Paleo-Indians would have found the mega-fauna (large prey) needed for their survival throughout the mountains up to Virginia, so in theory they would have been well within a premiere hunting range.

The Paleo-Indians, for all their 'primitive' stature in our eyes, made fine-quality tools and weapons, including Clovis type spear-points, a variety of knife-edged implements, and scrapers for cleaning animal skins. They appear to have made no pottery or other domestic accouterments, left no formal burials, constructed no shelters or otherwise left any indication of permanent settlement.

With the boreal forest at that stage in the mountain's history prevalent down to 2,000 feet on Grandfather's flanks, the so-called 'carrying capacity' of the area for more extensive human activity would have to be reckoned as very low, and unlikely to support anything in the nature of a permanent inhabited or habitable site. On Grandfather, scientifically extracted artifacts of paleolithic origin have been found throughout the mountain, mainly along Wilson's Creek and the Watauga and Linville Watersheds. Unfortunately, none have been recorded in undisturbed conjunction with any animal bones, charcoal, or other evidence of exactly what they were doing on the mountain. Also, the perishable nature of many of such finds, especially in acidic soil, make a lot of conclusions conjecture.

On the basis of the material analysis of these earliest remains that did survive, and in the continuity of their dated time of use, it would appear that Grandfather Mountain was a regular stop on the seasonal foraging cycle of the Paleo-Indians.

Like other animals, human nomads and migrants can roam over great distances but return to known locations whenever possible. Proof of this has been discovered in the High Country, most emphatically at the Watauga River Valley site at Cove Creek, in the form of a fortified 'proto-Cherokee' village. Likewise, along the river bottom terrain of nearby Ashe County, where gardens and plowed fields have yielded hundreds of artifacts representing thousands of years of abiding, if occasional, Paleo-Indian activity.

Somewhere around 10,000 B.P., a number of small but significant changes in the artifact record led archaeologists to introduce a new period into North American prehistory -- the Archaic. This era would last, with numerous 'phases' attached, for approximately 7,000 years.

One of these shifts involved the material most frequently employed for points in the Summit Region. Most prized had been the dark chert or flint found across the Continental Divide in what is now Tennessee, but the Archaic Period, characterized by tools and weapons suited to smaller game, saw increased use of quartz and quartzite. From Grandfather's Boone Fork Rock Shelter and richer sites in Virginia's Shenandoah Valley, archaeologists know that the base camps for the traveling bands were most often situated near quartz outcrops, quite sensibly as near as possible to their source of the core stone.

Grandfather's exposed rock features would have been a powerful attraction, even perhaps the one that first brought the foraging band up the creek.

Humans seemed to be, if not settling in, at least coming to more comfortable terms with their New World. The giant predators, mostly northern species like mammoth, saber-tooth tigers, et al, had been extinguished by hunting, warming climate and altered habitat. As the environment stabilized, so would the human population. They still roamed unsettled through the mountains, but in greater numbers, and security.

We can make an example of one object that points to a less precarious existence, the sandstone bowl. Commonly found in fragments throughout the region, and on Grandfather along the upper Watauga River, the humble stone bowl was used for

**The Crystal Mine.** A unique geological formation
of the Grandfather Window.

**Shanty Springs Branch.** Many of Grandfather's rare
threatened and endangered species inhabit the area of the branch.

**Grey's Lily.**

**Heller's Blazing Star.**

**Mountain Laurel.**

**Flame Azalea.**

PHOTO BY MILES TAGER

**Chestnut stump.**
Before a blight intro-
duced from Europe
the American
Chestnut was the
predominant hard-
wood species of the
Appalachians.

**Watauga River.**
"Sparkling clean water"
in the Cherokee lan-
guage, the Watauga is
one of two rivers whose
headwaters flow off
Grandfather Mountain.

PHOTO BY MILES TAGER

Rime frost at 5,000 feet up the north slope.

PHOTO BY MILES TAGER

**Northern flying squirrel.** Like many species this squirrel reaches the southern end of its breeding range on Grandfather Mountain.

**Yonahlossee salamander.** Grandfather has recorded more salamander species than any other single location in the United States.

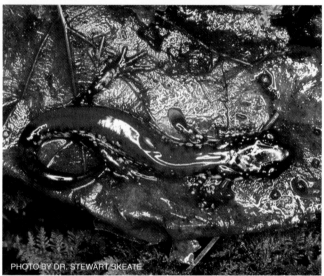

**Bobcat.** Not the largest feline predator in the region. Despite many sightings no known current photograph exists of the mountain lion, the top cat of the southern mountains.

**Raven.** Common at above 5,000 feet on Grandfather and other Appalachian peaks. Distinguished from its close cousin the crow by its 'boat' tail.

**Saw-whet owl.** Rare in the south, the owl has just been found to breed on Grandfather.

**Striped skunk.** One of two skunk species that can be found on the mountain.

**Before:** 1906; when Grandfather
sported its mantle of ancient forest.

**Price Lake.** A man-made lake adjoining Grandfather
and the Blue Ridge Parkway that attracts many water-
fowl rarely seen in the mountains.

**After:** 1995; Grandfather's forest is regrowing minus the Chestnut and with far less abundant Fraser fir.

This elk reintroduction on Grandfather failed miserably but represented the first such effort to reestablish a mammal species in America. The elk had been brought back to the Southeast from Yellowstone National Park.

**Daniel Boone.** His early exploits and explorations brought him repeatedly to hunting camps on Grandfather Mountain.

FROM 'DANIEL BOONE' BY JOHN MACK FARAGHER.
PAINTING BY JOHN JAMES AUDUBON

**Frenchman Andre Micheaux** *(right)* **and Philadelphia's William Bartram.** Two of the many noted scientists who conducted research on the mountain.

This road up to the summit
was later paved for the
booming tourist industry.

**Shull's Mill.** The north slope of Grandfather was heavily logged after the
turn of the century. One community, Linville, became known as 'Stumptown'.

**A View Forever.**
Man and mountaintop.

Grandmother Mountain, at left with TV tower, and Grandfather above the clouds that soak the Southern Appalachians.

cracking and grinding seeds, roots, and nuts. Easily worked out of the soft material common in the lower elevations, portable yet sturdy, these simple items represent the first manufactured domestic implement of the Appalachian Summit area, predating permanent houses to put them in.

Their key importance lies in that they replace a task previously accomplished with whatever materials were at hand, showing a commitment to the stability of place. This flashy new technology didn't just adapt to conditions, it planned for them, and went a long way toward determining, and finally, controlling them.

These archaic peoples also made grooved spear points and axe heads, a design innovation enabling a far securer attachment of the point to the haft or shaft with cured thong. Having a knife rather than serrated edge, the axes were now often polished with soapstone, another interesting development that had little practical purpose, but showed pride in workmanship. Another feature of steadily developing societies, this advance demonstrated not only the inclination, but the time needed away from mere survival to fashion beautiful things.

In addition to the raw material for tools and weapons, Grandfather also provided the hard, durable gneiss used by the Archaic peoples to shape their implements and weapons. Holding a quartz or quartzite core on an animal skin between their legs, the adept knapper, or tool-maker, would take these fist-sized 'hammer stones' and knock flakes off the core into the basic shape of a spear point or scraper. Once roughed out, the crafter would knock it into final form using a smaller stone held between thumb and two fingers. Finally, the very delicate work of shaping an even, razor sharp serrated cutting edge would be accomplished by 'pressure flaking' with an antler tip, pushing, rather than striking, tiny fragments off the tool edge.

These hammer stones were reused until badly pitted, then reused again as fire or boiling stones, where they were heated red-hot, then thrown into a skin-lined, water-filled pit or container to boil the water.

The Paleo-Indian and Archaic remains on Grandfather reveal not only its critical role as the origin for raw materials, but as a source and stop on a network of trade routes. For some of the artifacts found on the mountain, especially in the earlier period, were not made of these local stones, but of slate, rhyolite, andusite and chert common to locations from north to Virginia's Mount Rogers, west to Tennessee's Great Valley and east to the Piedmont of North Carolina.

The famous Hopewell Mounds in the Midwest contained mica mined from Mitchell County, North Carolina, just south of Grandfather. Similar mixes of material are found through the Summit Region, and beyond, although the finds show a increasing tendency by the Archaic bands to expand their horizons locally, by exploiting mostly regional resources.

As we watch our predecessors grow in numbers, skills, and sophistication, we must still remain frustrated in knowing much about *who* they were, the flesh on these bare bones. The one local site that might have brought them more to life, with potentially thousands of artifacts layered over possibly millennia of use, lies barren now on Grandfather Mountain.

Enough finds have been uncovered, from Linville to Julian Price Park, from Wilson's Creek on the south slope to the Watauga watershed on the north, to show that the mountain featured continually in the thousands of years of nomadic venturing. Some band or bands would have returned to the mountain on a regular basis, for stone, wood, bark, herbs, berries, fish, fowl, or game. But it wasn't until 1892 that the possible proof of this jumped out of the historical record, when someone noted a rare cave high up the northwest slope of Grandfather on the way to Attic Window Peak. Inside, its floor was littered with archeological evidence. Nothing like it had been discovered, or at least reported before in the area, where the hard metamorphosed Blue Ridge spine made cavern openings a rarity.

Now known as the Indian Rocks Cave, this dugout is more of an extended rock shelter than a true cave, and represented more of a way-station for prehistoric wanderers than a permanent occupation site.

Nevertheless, it proffered a unique glimpse into the past. Or might have; by 1951, when the cave came to the attention of the scientific community, investigations revealed that much of the evidence had already either been disrupted or been hauled away, leaving no additional clues to the status of our forebears.

Around 5,000 years ago, this peaceful (no evidence of warfare has been found during the Archaic Period) era in Grandfather's history began to come to an end, not in some cataclysmic event, but in slow transition far more earth-shaking in its consequences for human development. It may have occurred through growing population, or scarcity of game, or from the accumulated knowledge from thousands of years following seasonal changes and growing intimacy with the terrain.

Ironically, this evolution in our behavior came about just as humans seem to have perfected their hunting (the bow and arrow having been invented) and gathering skills. But for whatever reasons, humans from this time on would not be content to live in harmony with natural cycles, but would be intent on mastering them.

The defining moment of the transition came when someone planted a seed, probably corn, cultivated it and harvested something to eat. The months of care needed to prepare the ground and nurture the crop required a radically different lifestyle, a permanent presence, a *home*. This in turn demanded entirely new skills, new tools, and a new outlook on life.

The hunt and the forest bounty had always been taken communally, shared on communal ground. But the homestead and crop belonged to the family or individual, not the tribe. As survival became more a matter of individual rather than group effort, the fruits of those labors became not *ours*, but *mine*.

The coming of settlement brought astonishing developments. A hungry wolf wandering into the clearing at night was not shot or chased away, but fed, then tamed, then trained. Perhaps most important, food and water had to be stored and saved for the long-term instead of just found and immediately consumed.

The transition from hunter-gatherer to farmer, from nomad to settler, is regarded by many scholars as still the most pivotal in all human development.

Not that life on Grandfather Mountain changed overnight. All the early 'Woodland Period' settlements were built in the flat alluvial river plains below the slopes, and of course foraging parties still came up the mountain for many of the traditional necessities of life. The first site previewing this new era was discovered along the lower Watauga River, and dated from between 5,000 and 3,000 B.P. While not precisely a settlement, i.e. having no permanent structures, it showed substantial sign of food storage and appropriate implements, including grinding stones, bowl fragments, and charred shell.

The earliest genuine occupation site near the mountain was unearthed at present-day Burnsville, in a fertile valley about fifty miles from Grandfather, and estimated at between 2,700 and 3,000 years old.

Technological advances leapfrogged during this Woodland Period, especially in ceramics. Decorated pottery appeared in the region around 2,300 B.P., soon followed by sand-tempered ware -- for greater durability -- flared rims and footed storage vessels for greater handling ease.

Around 2,000 B.P. signs of commerce with the highly developed Ohio River Valley (Hopewellian) Culture appeared. The Hopewellians were the most advanced North American culture of the time, living in large stockaded towns, and farming and trading extensively.

Raw materials from the Grandfather Mountain environ, including mica, quartzite, and possibly copper, were now being bartered and used many hundreds of miles from the source. One thousand years later, archaeologists recognized the distinctive 'Mississippian' Period throughout the southeast United States, a stable domestic culture featuring decorative art on a variety of media, and extremely fine micro-tool technology. In the mountains, only scattered evidence has been found of this last prehistoric period before the modern time, indications of the people sometimes referred to as the Proto-Cherokee.

This was the successful civilization discovered four hundred years later when heavily armed and armored troops under Hernando De Soto hacked their way up from Florida into the North Carolina mountains. As recorded today, the people the Conquistadores encountered were called the Cherokee Indians.

How or when the Cherokee evolved during this era is unknown. (The word *Cherokee* is of European origin; the indigenous Indians, here as in many other cultures, referred to themselves simply as 'The People'. One very key question about the origin of the Cherokee, one that DNA research may finally unlock, returns to the beginning of the Indian tribes themselves. Many pre-historians believe that tribal divisions started to occur somewhere in the time of the so-called Pisgah Culture, between 800 B.P. and the coming of the whites. The tribes may have evolved from their distinct environments into separate ethnic peoples, or have established fluid but distinct identities within the same racial framework. The precise how or why of this process awaits, or possibly confounds, future research.)

Common wisdom has long held the Cherokee to be of Iroquoian ancestry, the southernmost of a tribally divided but racially unified people that stretched from the Midwest to the Eastern Seaboard, and the Canadian border to the Alabama foothills. If there is a chance the Southern Appalachians were first populated by pilgrims from South America, by a race of unclear origin and development, perhaps it is the Iroquois who are of Cherokee derivation.

Numbers represent another quandary. The most oft-repeated figure for the Cherokee population of the Appalachian Summit Region -- when De Soto's troops entered the picture -- is about 22,000. Based on available evidence, or lack of it, one can probably regard this or any other estimate with equal skepticism. But some researchers now believe that estimates of pre-colonization native populations have been wildly underestimated, perhaps by a factor of ten.

Even having developed into a secure farming culture, the Cherokee still shared the hunting and warrior traditions of their forebears. From earliest records, archeological and historical, they fought the Catawba Indians, residents of the foothills and Piedmont to the south and east of Cherokee territory. But Indians did not fight to acquire territory. Although some material gain like horses, slaves, or hides might be garnered from victory over one's enemies, the primary point of these tribal enmities seems to have been the victory itself, proof, perhaps, of the superiority of "The People".

Despite their predilection for farming and village life, the Cherokee were fearsome hunters. In their Creation myth, the first man, *Karati*, was a hunter, while his mate *Selu* gave birth to the corn and other crops. Like virtually all Native Americans, the Cherokee tribal order mirrored this ancient division of labor by gender. Wearing deerskin camouflage, including head and antlers, the men hunted with spears and spear throwers, bow and arrow, and blowgun.

They employed many strategies, including the use of deadfalls, decoys, and herding. They fished the trout streams of the mountains with baskets and trot lines, nets, spears, traps, and bare hands, and even used a concoction of the medicine men, an herbal sedative, to throw in the river pools to stun the fish. They were expert, also, in leaving enough to sustain future generations, both of hunter and prey.

The Cherokee were no less proficient in the old ways of gathering wild bounty. On the high peaks like Roan and Grandfather, they foraged, men and women alike, for nuts, berries, and more than 500 plant species used by the tribe to produce food, medicine, dye, ceremony, and magic. Many of these items were to be found only at the highest elevations. The barks of the Fraser Fir and Red Spruce, for example, were stripped and cured for their widespread medicinal properties, then applied as a salve, poultice, tonic, or tea.

Passed on to the white settlers, and led by the potent ginseng root (which the Cherokee revered as a living spirit, calling him the Little Man), the herbal lore of the region has been well-studied and documented. But some of the more esoteric functions of the rich mythic life surrounding the Cherokee have received less attention, or kept better secret by their elders.

Herbs could be applied not only for physical healing, but for more otherworldly transformations as well. The highly publicized peyote ceremonies of the American West have their counterparts in all indigenous peoples. Medicine men from the Australian outback to the African jungle to the Blue Ridge High Country have used mind-altering substances to produce visions, knowledge, and power. And in such a rich bio-region as the Appalachians, they found no shortage of raw materials; jimson weed, cannabis, and species of mushroom and fungi with hallucinogenic properties.

In non-Western societies, spiritual life and practical life are inseparable, indeed, indistinguishable. Every significant time, place, and activity exists in both real and dream time. Each everyday event has a sacred counter life, represented by a ceremony; the ceremony confirms that every day *is* sacred. But some are more sacred, more powerful, than others.

In the natural world the mountain lion is more powerful than the hare. If not more important (Indians knew instinctively that predators cannot exist without prey), the cougar was more revered, an imposing creature and spirit alike. The cat's mythic power matched its dominance of the mountains.

Many cultures esteemed one creature above all, the most powerful of both the animal kingdom and the netherworld. The Cherokee held the eagle in this regard, as did ultimately even their conquerors who made the Bald Eagle their national symbol. The tribe, or its shadowy predecessors, had also accorded rank of power to places as well as animals, a rank likewise based on function and form, physical and metaphysical presence.

The eagle spirit may have ranged all over earth and sky but he needed a nest, a location so secret it was known only to the highest medicine man, a place that alone in all the Cherokee domain carried the name of *Tanawha*, the Fabulous Eagle. That place was Grandfather Mountain.

Beyond the honor of the name, the exact nature of Grandfather's role in Cherokee mythology, as in their lives, will probably never be deciphered, if it is even now remembered. One theory holds that the mountain contained the entrances to the underworld. These were reputed to be as numerous as the spring heads that marked their opening, and accessible to worthy soul searchers. Admission could be granted (and return guaranteed) to those who could keep both the location and the experience a secret. The guardians of both were the 'little people', denizens of forest mythologies everywhere.

The similarities of Native American to Celtic, Arabic and other legendary versions of these little folk are truly compelling. In most instances they share the characteristic personae of sometimes playful, sometimes dangerous, but always willful and unpredictable. They like riddles, and like children, can change shape, moods and allegiances instantly. In the Cherokee lexicon, as in many others, anyone who revealed the entrance or wonders of the underworld would be struck dumb, or dead.

The underworld perhaps boasted another, more fearsome keeper. According to white interpretation of legend, unauthorized entry would be met by the form of a black panther who filled up the spring head with his own. A black cat: where in Appalachia had the Indians encountered a black panther? In modern times they hadn't, but if we return to the question of their origin, we can pause to consider that the black jaguar is endemic to the south and central Americas, and although not now known north of the American southwest, may represent the forerunner of the present mountain lion.

Aside from its physical domination of the landscape, we do know of one unique aspect of Grandfather's makeup that accounts for its high status in the mythic pantheon of the Cherokee; that of a source for quartz crystals.

Perhaps one misty morning on the mountain revealed not a native hunting party, but a lone figure headed high up the north slope. As the sun burns off the swirled shroud high among the balsams, we spot an elderly man, moving slowly among the rock fall. He will be making for the crystal mine, hidden by thick stands of spruce-fir, but known to this medicine man as the source of one of his most precious possessions.

Pure quartz crystals made magic, but in the interlock between everyday and otherworldly, were used by the Cherokee shamans for eminently practical purposes, specifically, to predict the future. The medicine men, the only tribal members allowed to find or handle these gems, would be consulted before one of several big occasions; a battle, recovery from a serious illness, a hunt, the question of a wife's faithfulness. In the presence of the beseecher, the wizard would peer into the stone for his (women were apparently excluded from this service) reflection.

If the man appeared in the stone standing upright, all would be well, and a lucky hunter, fearless warrior, or grateful husband could then proceed. But if the figure cast in the crystal lay prone, doom was equally assured. In this instance, a warrior could actually beg off a battle, knowing he would die, without seeming a coward. The stand-up braves would feel invulnerable, and face their dangers without fear.

These crystals were treated as living beings by the Cherokee, and they consequently had to be fed, preferably with the blood of deer. If they were not, the stones tended to wander in search of food, and eat what they could, posing a serious threat to animals and humans alike. Like many species, they became bad tempered when hungry. Even the medicine men had to handle them with great care, wrapping them in a deerskin pouch soaked in blood, not touching them with bare fingers.

One of the greatest figures in Cherokee mythology, the giant snake *Uktena*, was covered with crystal scales, and derived its powers from a single crystal embedded in its forehead. This stone was a perfect quartz crystal shot through with deep-red filaments like fire, or blood. For the Cherokee, the red threads meant that the stone was feeding internally, and eternally, on deer blood, giving it an infinite energy source. This rendered it the most powerful object in creation. Only the highest shaman could survive contact with these stones.

This type of gem still exists, and is known to us as rutilated quartz. Rutile is a titanium crystal that often appears within other stones, especially gneiss. The primary source for rutilated quartz in the region lies in Alexander County, North Carolina, in the foothills of the Blue Ridge just thirty miles southeast of Grandfather Mountain. For as long as there have been Cherokee, this area has been held in the domain of their bitterest enemies, the Catawba Tribe, and we can only speculate whether another, secret source existed within their own territory, perhaps on Grandfather itself.

Of all the great events, large and small, occurring on the mountain, these happening in the Indian dream time will likely remain matters of speculation. Their myth and lore that has passed on to the modern time seems extensive, but was coaxed from elders by well-meaning whites who had trouble with both the language and concepts of what they were told. There was also the Indians' tendency to feed these insistent questioners a line, either as a joke, or for the most serious reason of leading them away from the tribe's greatest secrets.

If any of the ancient shamanist ways survive, if the spring heads and crystal mines on Grandfather could reveal more than meets the eye, they are being held secret still.

# CHAPTER 4

## *Explorations*

They came first looking for gold. A few hundred men, covered in and carrying metal, blundering through the rhododendron and laurel hells of the seemingly endless forest. What could the Cherokee have thought of this column of men whose clothing glinted in the sunlight, whose blades could cut off branches and heads, who fired exploding sticks, and marched with a herd of a thousand swine?

The year was 1540, and the column was led by the Spaniard Hernando de Soto. They had already tramped through a thousand miles of swamp and savannah, and their search would now take them through the mountains all the way across the Mississippi River to Oklahoma.

De Soto's exact route through the Appalachians is still being debated, but it is generally accepted he first encountered the Cherokee in the Balsam Mountains near Franklin, North Carolina, about a hundred miles southwest of Grandfather Mountain. The Spanish did not tarry but continued west, no doubt encouraged by the local Indians that whatever they were looking for was to be found far from them.

De Soto had no interest in colonizing such a wild realm so removed from his dreamscape of gold, and his passing left the land and people of the mountains largely unscathed. It would be almost two centuries before the bulk of the colonists followed in his wake.

Some venturesome individuals did, however, come up the rivers, likely the Yadkin and Catawba, to the high peaks of the Blue Ridge. By the late 1600's, Grandfather had once again become a fixture in an ancient activity -- trade -- with a new twist. These new traders were mainly French explorers trapping for animal pelts to sell in the growing settlements back east, and to adorn the wealthy in London and Paris.

The Cherokee wondered, at first, why these explorers took not what they needed, but as much or more as they could carry.

Like De Soto, the early trappers came and went, leaving only the puzzle of their ways.

The turn of the century brought a different and distinct breed to the mountain, indeed, one of the most remarkable race of folk in American history.

Ships were now plying the Atlantic between the Old World and the established settlements in Virginia and the Carolinas, bringing Europe's flintiest souls to the 'new' continent. While many had ventured into the wilderness, few had yet dared live in it. The English pilgrims in particular considered the dark woods filled with savage beasts and painted naked humans as the work of the Devil.

However, some of the earliest colonials were outcasts of a different stripe. To them the wilderness represented a refuge from persecution which had followed their wanderings throughout all of Europe, and had continued in the towns of the New World. These people were the Melungeons.

The first Melungeon to tread on American soil is believed to be one Captain Juan Pardo, who landed in South Carolina in 1580. Hired on by the Spanish as a ship's pilot (as were many 'Portagee' in the days of sail), he came ashore at the Spanish military outpost near Parris Island, South Carolina, established fourteen years before.

In 1581 Pardo led a contingent of soldiers into the interior. He built small forts and left garrisons in a line from upstate South Carolina to northeast Tennessee, then, apparently abandoning the garrisons, returned to the coast. Those garrison men, numbering perhaps a hundred or so, were ostensibly never heard from again.

But a century later, French traders brought back tales to the settlements of a raucous rag-tag group of half-wild men and women, in the highest, wildest corners of the uplands, living in the lee of Grandfather Mountain. Some of the trappers thought they must be apparitions, not surprising considering they described a race of olive-skinned, black-haired, blue-eyed Europeans who spoke a dialect of Elizabethan English, called themselves 'Portyghee', and inhabited a place hundreds of miles from the nearest outposts of civilization.

The French consulted the Cherokee, who assured them these creatures existed, but were devils, and that they would have nothing to do with them. Like the Indians, the French gave them a wide berth whenever possible, and the Melungeons would have the High Country much to themselves for a few decades more. They scratched out an existence in the back "hollers" of what are now Watauga, Avery, Ashe, and Yancey counties, reportedly gambling, fighting, inbreeding and making moonshine.

And so was born the stereotype of the Appalachian hillbilly.

Between incidents of reputed low behavior, the Melungeons also farmed, mined various minerals, made tools, fine decorative metalwork and jewelry, and established the earliest European settlements in the mountains of North Carolina and Tennessee.

By the early 1700's, settlers were pouring into the settlements, now cities, of the coastal plan, and spilling over into the Piedmont and foothills throughout the southeast. The mountains were next. Hunting parties and other expeditions regularly came up the many rivers to Grandfather and throughout the region, and the large numbers of immigrant highland Scots-Irish eyed this terrain as fine territory to settle in. The Cherokee at this stage posed little threat to colonization; indeed they lived much as the newcomers intended, farming, hunting, gathering, trading, and living in small, self-sustaining communities. They were generally peaceful unless roused, and usually eager to accept the white men's ways, especially those made of metal.

The Melungeons, on the other hand, secretive and hostile to civilization, would have to go. And so they did. Despite their reputation for violence, the Melungeons tended to avoid confrontation, showing every indication of just wishing to be left alone. As the Scots-Irish filtered into the Grandfather region, the Melungeons moved on, taking the traditional route from the mountain, the Watauga River, west into Tennessee. Here they finally settled for good.

The Tennessee towns of Watauga and Elizabethton today clearly reveal the ancestors of the Melungeons in the faces of their inhabitants, Caucasian features set in wide faces, dark skin and hair. The only traces they appear to have left on Grandfather Mountain were their names on headstones; Goins, Collins, Gibson, and Mullins. The last Melungeon, Vandy Collins, left the region for Tennessee in 1830. Their origins remain murky, and laced with the fantastic. Destined forever to be outcasts, the Melungeons wandered from North Africa to Portugal to the Carolina coast and across the Blue Ridge via Grandfather Mountain.

The name Melungeon derives either from the French, 'melange', or mixture, or the Portugese 'melango', or shipmate. Mixture they certainly were, to such a degree that they have been variously labeled the survivors of the sunken city of Atlantis or the Lost Tribe of Israel; described as Black Dutch, as well as Black Irish. In fact, recent DNA testing reveals their bloodlines (believed to number about 100,000) to be no less exotic than the tales surrounding them: their stock includes Portugese, Spanish, Berber, Arab, Jewish, African, and Cherokee.

By the mid-1700's the Scots-Irish had consolidated their claim to the Appalachian mountains south of Virginia, and were setting about civilizing them.

Charles Linville wasn't looking for gold, game or refuge. He was looking for Indians, to kill them. It was 1766. Bearing over the Grandfather Mountain, up the river that took his name, Linville and a small band of armed men crossed the Blue Ridge escarpment from the east. They clashed with a party of Cherokee, and in the ensuing skirmish Linville was killed. Buried in a forgotten grave somewhere on the mountain, Linville became the first European known to have been killed west of the Blue Ridge Mountains and the Eastern Divide.

Trouble had already been brewing between Indians and whites, over (what else?) land. The first official government act pertaining to the area had been passed three years earlier by the British Colonial Administration, banning settlement beyond the Divide and setting all the lands west aside for the Indians. This had not set well with Charles Linville and many other settlers.

By 1776 the first regional outpost, and westernmost in the territories, had been established at Old Fort, North Carolina, at the foot of the mountains less than a hundred miles south of Grandfather. With revolution brewing behind, the advance columns of pioneers were in no mood for holding back; the continent lay there for the taking. When the British and their set-aside law were finally overthrown, the last obstacle to the land rush was cast aside. By the end of the war, settlers had bought, claimed, staked, homesteaded or just plain stolen all the land drained by the Watauga River, including Grandfather's north slope from Linville Gap to Boone.

These early developments did not end the isolation of the mountain region, however. The Scots-Irish mountaineers had no particular love for any government or their tax men, and the great wagon trains of pioneers heading west were taking the far less rigorous routes to the north. Although contained within one of the original thirteen colonies, North Carolina's Blue Ridge frontier bore little resemblance to its civilized counterpart back east, which would establish the nation's first state university at Chapel Hill in 1789, and statehood two years later.

For some, the romantic notion of self-sufficiency and independence soon dissipated under the hardships of frontier survival, not least of which was the rapidly disappearing wildlife. In the first flush of independence and land acquisition, over 500 settlers registered as inhabitants of what is roughly now Avery County, containing the bulk of Grandfather Mountain. Ten years later, just thirteen families remained.

Trade routes to the coast had been long established, existing mainly to take out the pelts, ginseng, and other items the mountains had to offer. But the mountain folk were too few and too poor to justify a return trade in the bounty of civilized society. The Appalachians remained isolated and 'primitive', living as the Cherokee, not only in the woods, but on the woods.

Here in this realm grew true abundance. Giants of trees 200 ft. tall and 8 ft. in diameter towered everywhere on and around the mountain, providing for their homes, barns, fences, wagons, furniture and firewood. The local chestnut, locust and white pine were discovered to be virtually rot and weather proof. The white pine in particular, light, soft, strong, stable, and easily worked, was highly prized, and taken out first.

Barns made of chestnut, and survey stakes of locust, would last hundreds of years in the damp climate. The red and white oaks, poplars, and maples made sturdy flooring and furniture, and the rich cherry and walnut wood provided the settlers with materials for fine cabinets and trim.

From the Cherokee, the settlers learned to make canoes from the beautiful stands of white birch that graced the mid-level slopes of Grandfather, and to use, not discard, the barks of the other trees they cut, for medicinal purposes.

The nut-bearing trees -- oaks, chestnut, butternut, hickory, and walnut -- saw many a family through the winters, complementing their diet of wild game, and providing mast for those animals as well. Ironically, as the Cherokee were assimilating the ways of lowland traders, that is to profit from mountain harvests even if it meant depleting the source, the early settlers were learning the opposite; that self-sufficiency meant leaving enough for next time.

Some of the uses the inhabitants derived from local raw materials became part and parcel of American culture, and remain in effect today. As they learned to strip and process the bark of the red spruce trees, it apparently occurred to some curious soul that the exposed resin must have tonic properties as well. The resin could be chewed as it was for sore throats and stomach ailments. Later it was flavored, and marketed, as chewing gum.

The eastern hemlock, another northern species growing to epic proportions at this southern end of its range, produced tan bark that processed out to the curative tannin, the staple preservative for making leather, or soft deerskin.

From the witch-hazel, the settlers extracted a multiple-use disinfectant that could be taken as a gargle, a drink for internal ulcers or bleeding, or applied externally for wounds. Two hundred years of progress has hardly improved on this elixir, as evidenced by its sale in every drugstore in the country. A wintergreen flavoring could be distilled from birch twigs, and wild cherry bark made the best cough medicine. The raison d'etre pharmaceutical cough syrups of today are still often cherry flavored.

The forest's understory made no less a contribution to the native's health and welfare. As modern medicine 'discovers' miracle cures in the tropical rainforests, many old-timers in the southern highlands will remember, and still use, the bounty close at hand; sassafras, comfrey, bloodroot, goldenseal, mandrake, coltsfoot, lady's-slipper, catnip, teaberry, chicory, and of course, ginseng.

The first actual home recorded anywhere on Grandfather Mountain cropped up around the year 1800, a hermit's cabin built along the Shanty Spring Branch on the north slope. His name and residence have long disappeared.

High-elevation shelters dotted the mountain's slopes from the earliest forays to take advantage of the game traveling the high ridges and outcrops, and sheltering in the protected coves and watersheds. Some traces of these remain, but no record exists of their occupants, with one notable exception. History does relate the tales of one frontiersman who built a rough hunting cabin on the mountain, a man by the name of Daniel Boone. Even if many of the fabulous stories told about Boone were apocryphal, he nevertheless well-deserves his legendary status among American pioneers.

Born in Pennsylvania in 1734, Boone settled along the Yadkin River in Rowan County, North Carolina, in 1751. At the age of 17 he was already a successful professional hunter. He first crossed the Blue Ridge on a hunting trip in 1760. He moved closer to the mountains and their still plentiful game (and as he would repeatedly do so, away from people and civilization) to near Wilkesboro, North Carolina, six years later.

Even after he moved to Kentucky to found the Boonesborough settlement, he returned to hunt and live in the state, in seasonal cabins throughout the Watauga River watershed, including the one on Grandfather Mountain. While Daniel passed through, his son was to settle on the mountain, building a home along a branch which came to be called Boone's Fork.

The hunting party that first introduced Boone to the high country was led by a freed black slave, and took him to a cabin in a remote upland meadow. Its location described only as near the sources of the New, Yadkin, and Watauga Rivers, this spot became his home away from home for ten years. So taken with it was Boone that he proposed to his wife Rebecca that they move there permanently. Mrs. Boone did not share her husband's need for isolation, and refused.

Although his prowess and success as a hunter were undeniable, the sheer numbers of game available for the taking, and taking for granted, we can scarcely imagine; an average hunter could, and did, kill up to five deer a day, and not many fewer black bear. Boone did not kill for sport.

One of his lesser known exploits probably had the greatest impact on American history. Returning to Piedmont North Carolina during the Revolutionary War, Boone was sought out as the country's foremost frontiersman to take a small contingent of non-combatants out of the war zone. He led the party of 100 out of danger across the mountains. One of the couples, Thomas and Nancy Hanks Lincoln, settled in Hardin County (now Larue County), Kentucky, where she would bear their son, Abraham.

Like so many other larger than life figures, Boone's numerous real adventures paled in the public's eye before those falsely assigned to him. His early upbringing in Pennsylvania included the non-violent tenets of the Quakers, and if he took neither that nor any other religion to church, he did take it to heart, and was never known to kill human or animal without reason.

He was much more prone to hunting with the Cherokee than hunting for them. As a professional hunter and tracker, he lived more like an Indian than an educated colonial, and he came to adapt their techniques, and finally to resemble one as well. He let his hair grow long, dressed it with bear grease, and plaited it into braids or knots. He wore breechclout and leggings, sometimes painting his body and performing other rituals before a hunt. After the kill, sitting around the campfire or in his cabin high up on Grandfather Mountain, Daniel Boone would amaze his company, white, black, Cherokee, and Melungeon, with another skill; he would pull out a book and read aloud. The two volumes which generally accompanied him to the wilds were the *Holy Bible* and Jonathan Swift's *Gulliver's Travels*.

This literacy is the key to exposing the myth of one of the most persistent tales about Boone, that he went about boasting of his bear kills by carving his name on a nearby tree. These scratchings, including one preserved along the lower Watauga River, claimed D. BOON KILLED A BAR, followed by the date. They are fake, or the work of another man. Even if Boone were to use the vernacular for 'bear', he most certainly would not have misspelled his name.

Boone's relationship with the Cherokee mirrors that of many frontier folk and the history of that time and place. The tolerance and even friendship that developed between individuals strained under the weight, and wont, of the growing white population. The two cultures never broke out into full-scale warfare, but even as he was being welcomed into their company in the mountains, Boone records Cherokee raids on white settlements along the Yadkin and Catawba Rivers in 1759. Sporadic skirmishing and violence erupted throughout the traditional Indian domain until a peace treaty was signed in 1760. Much of the Cherokee anger had been ignited by a smallpox epidemic that killed off approximately half the entire tribe in 1750. The game was disappearing as well; as early as 1753, thirty thousand deerskins were exported from North Carolina alone.

In the high country, avengers of Charles Linville struck back shortly after his death, drumming up a large posse and once again crossing the divide, driving Chief Estatoe and his small band out of Burnsville and the region for good.The straw that broke the Cherokee back, and sent most of them down the Trail of Tears in 1840, were little pieces of paper called land deeds. The first land-grant recorded on Grandfather Mountain by the new American government was registered in the Shull's Mill area on the lower northwest slope in 1788.

During the early 1800's, white immigration to the region remained a trickle compared to the flood engulfing other more accessible and arable territory to the north and south. The hardy few who did first settled the High Country, Scots-Irish with names like Calloway and McClurd, hacked out the first road between 1815 and 1830. It ran along the south side of the

Watauga River, connecting Boone and Burnsville through the Linville Gap at the base of Grandfather's north side.

The rocky soil and steep slopes discouraged large crop farming, but the settlers did plant small orchards and vegetables gardens. They kept cattle, pigs, and sheep, and bartered, hunted, and gathered. They produced a single cash crop, moonshine, that brought them into contact with the outside world. For most of the 18th century, the burgeoning population of America passed the mountains by, with one exception.

A select group of adventurers did ascend the Blue Ridge, and Grandfather Mountain in particular, during the pioneer era of the 1800's. They toted notebooks, field glasses and specimen containers instead of land titles. Although tiny in numbers, these few scientists were to put this back country into the forefront of at least a corner of the national stage. Even before 1800, the urbanization of eastern America was growing at a pace that drove men like Daniel Boone further into the wilderness.

In most of Europe, the great forests and beasts of the forests had disappeared centuries before, and tales of the American wild piqued more than a little interest among men hungry for knowledge as well as those hungry for gold or land.

A century before a gentleman renegade by the name of Charles Darwin sailed off to the Galapagos Islands on *HMS Beagle*, American natural science and natural history were being born in the back country of North Carolina.

# CHAPTER 5

## *Explanations*

"It abounds with curiosities worthy a nice observation."

*-John Lawson*

John Lawson was the Surveyor-General of the Carolina Territories, an esteemed position in the early 1700's, when division and acquisition of lands defined the very nature of the infant country. What truly set Lawson apart from his compatriots, those looking for a material stake in the New World, was not great intellect or a higher environmental awareness. Although he could be said now to possess those traits, what drove Larson to become the first natural scientist on American soil was no more than basic driving curiosity. He loved, above all, a 'nice observation'.

As a surveyor, he traveled widely. As he wrote down his bearings and angles, he noted his surroundings as well, in particular the quantity and quality of the wildlife. Away from the coastal settlements, both were abundant. Wolves, Lawson wrote, "go in great droves by night", and he recorded common sightings of cougar, beaver, turkey, and great flocks of both game and non-game birds. The herds of bison, however, prime hunting targets, he noticed were already becoming a rarity.

This simple recording of the numbers, location, and decline of species represented a revolutionary departure from the overriding cultural bias toward nature; a murky swirl of fear and exploitation. Lawson's gentle observations were farsighted acts in themselves, but, based on his field experience with animal behavior, he stepped beyond mere data collection to challenge the notion that wild nature represented an essential threat to human existence.

He claimed that the great wolfpacks "are not man-slayers, neither is any creature in Carolina unless wounded." This statement alone placed him far enough out of the mainstream to amount to heresy, and landed him a place in the annals of science. In 1711 Lawson undertook a thousand mile survey through the Carolinas, leaving Currituck Sound, North Carolina and heading due west, turning aside beneath the Blue Ridge, then proceeding south by southeast to the low country of South Carolina. Some historians place his westerly progress as falling well short of the mountains, somewhere around the present city of High Point, North Carolina. But Lawson records "the most amazing prospect I had seen since I had been in Carolina; there appearing great ridges of mountains bearing from us W.N.W. One alp with a top like a sugar-loaf advanced its head above all the rest very considerably...these mountains were clothed all over with trees, which seem'd to be very large Timbers."

This perspective would place Lawson much closer to the escarpment than High Point, but whatever the mountain he encountered, this passage exemplifies a problem common to many of the early explorations; without names or other guidelines the descriptions of place are maddeningly inexact. Anyone attempting to exactly retrace Lawson's, DeSoto's, or subsequent early explorer's routes through the mountains have failed to do so, and they are still being debated today.

Lawson's record of his journey, *The History of North Carolina*, was the first such documentation and the first natural history printed on the American continent. In breaking such new ground, Lawson found the lack of animal classification, like mountains without names, to be a serious impediment. The brilliant work of the Swedish botanist Carolus Linnaeus, allowing naturalists a system to work under, was years off yet, and Lawson had found numerous animals unknown in Europe. One of them was a species of tortoise. Lawson knew snakes and frogs to be reptiles, but he had never heard of a member of this family with a shell. So he decided, unhappily, that it must something else; ...tortoise, vulgarly called Turtle: "I have ranked these among the insects because they lay eggs, and I did not know well where to put them..."

This miscalculation aside, Lawson's viewpoints set the standard for further research, sparking the next torch-bearer to conduct his investigations in the Carolinas, to take his work deeper and higher into the wild country, and onto Grandfather Mountain.

Mark Catesby arrived in Virginia in 1712, an opportune time to pick up where Lawson had left off. An avid student of botany and zoology, Catesby collected specimens as he traveled through the Tidewater of the Old Dominion. By 1722 he had raised the financial backing necessary to compile his data into a book of his own, and to venture further, beyond Lawson, into the mountains.

Lawson had simply recorded what he had happened upon; Catesby went deliberately in search of the unknown. And he added another dimension to the field of natural science; he was a gifted illustrator, and would sketch, as well as describe, what he found.

He set out that spring for Cherokee country, and aided by the Indians, (whom he said were particularly enamored of his drawing abilities) brought back to civilization the first detailed record of the flora and fauna of southern Appalachia. He drew fish, fowl, plant, animal, and human, and over a hundred species of birds.

He advanced two daring theories based on his observations. The first related to the disappearance of many species of birds in the winter. Accepted hypothesis for this mysterious event was at the time that the immense flocks of swifts, pigeons, songbirds et. al. hided off to some nether region for the cold months, and buried themselves in the mud. It was even suggested that the millions of passenger pigeons could only be accommodated out of sight on an undiscovered moon.

Watching chimney swifts, Catesby postulated instead that these birds 'migrated' south. Many species, he felt, should be considered "birds of passage" who "pass to the same latitude in the southern hemisphere from whence they came."

More far-reaching still, Catesby presented an explanation for the dark-skinned races of the Americas; that they descended from Asiatic origins and crossed a land-bridge across the narrowest point between the continents, the Bering Strait, sometime in the distant past.

Two hundred years would pass before archaeological evidence was uncovered that could confirm this idea, an imaginative leap without precedent in the science of his time. If

Lawson predated him in exploration and publication, Catesby is rightly acknowledged as the pioneer botanist, ornithologist, anthropologist and wildlife artist in American history.

He visited Grandfather Mountain during the expedition of 1722, the first to cross the Blue Ridge Mountains. He brought back the first evidence of exotic species like ginseng, trillium, and the ruffed grouse. He remarked on herds of elk, who "usually accompany bufaloes, with whom they range in the upper and remote parts of Carolina."

Catesby published his definitive volume of work in 1732. As natural history was hardly a household term, he named his book accordingly: *Being a Natural History of Carolina, Florida, and the Bahama Islands, containing the Figures of Birds, Beasts, Fishes, Serpents, Insects, and Plants. To which are added, Observations on the Air, Soil, and Water, with Remarks upon Agriculture, Grain, Pulse, Roots, etc.*

This tome commanded attention on both sides of the Atlantic, inspiring not only additional research, but the notion of organized, funded scientific expeditions. Credit Catesby as well with foreshadowing the work of John James Audubon, who adapted and perfected his technique of painting birds and mammals against their natural background. Natural historians have often wondered why the inveterate wanderer Audubon never once set foot in North Carolina; perhaps it was because he considered Catesby's work so definitive.

Prominent among American scientists who did follow Catesby's footsteps to the Blue Ridge, and to Grandfather, was William Bartram. Bartram came from an elite cultured background, his father a renowned Philadelphia botanist, and a student who wore out his original edition of Catesby's *Natural History.*

In 1775 he set off on his first expedition, often closely following Catesby's route. He headed to Florida first, but acknowledged in his journals that as fascinating as the sub-tropics might be, he was less than captivated by the insects, and the 'dreadful' alligators. Like Catesby, he found the Cherokee and Cherokee country to be delightful, the 'western mountains' especially welcome after the heat of the swamps.

He climbed Grandfather Mountain in 1776, noting and gathering numerous specimens, many not recorded by Catesby. Back in Philadelphia, Bartram sorted his notes and finds at the Deales Museum, the first in the nation devoted to natural history. Here he was privileged to work with many of the most prodigious scientific minds of the era: Benjamin Franklin, Thomas Jefferson, Alexander Wilson and the Audubons. Bartram published his *Travels through North and South Carolina* in 1791. He listed 215 species of birds, the most ever recorded by a single observer at the time.

Bartram brought to the field, and to the Grandfather region, something that Lawson and Catesby had been unable to accomplish -- international recognition. This was due partly to his family's connections, and the corresponding wide distribution of his book.

But Bartram also achieved his measure of success honestly, by the power of his fine descriptive writing. He inspirited many who read his work with the poetry as well as the salience of the American wilderness. *Travels* was not only praised by scientists and statesmen, but by writers like Carlyle, Coleridge, and Wordworth. Rare in a scientist, Bartram could entwine his facts with haunting evocations, capturing both the nature and spirit of his subject.

Among his very fine subjects were the Flame Azalea, a riotous upland species that he named and first catalogued on Grandfather and other high peaks. He made the most of his material:

> The epithet *fiery* I annex to this celebrated species of azalea...of the color of the finest red, lead, orange, and bright gold as well as yellow and cream...not only in separate plants but frequently all the varieties and shades in separate branches on the same plant; and the clusters of blossoms cover the shrubs in such incredible profusion on the hillside that suddenly opening to view from dark shades we are alarmed with apprehension of the hill being set on fire. This is certainly the most brilliant flowering shrub yet known...

Almost two centuries later, the noted writer and activist Edward Abbey returned to Appalachia with Bartram's words in his heart:

In trying to imagine what our country must have been like two hundred years ago, before the black plague of commerce, industrialism, and urbanism laid its fatal curse upon the land, we could do worse than review what appeared to the candid eyes of such an honest observer as William Bartram. The landscape of the southern Appalachians looked like this in 1773; 'I traveled some miles over a varied situation of ground, exhibiting views of grand forests, dark, detached groves, vales, and meadows. Crossed a delightful river, began to ascend again, first over swelling turfy ridges, varied with groves of stately forest trees, then ascending more steep and grassy hillsides.'

With both the region and the discipline of naturalism established as areas of prime importance, Grandfather Mountain and environs now drew attention, and scientists, from around the world.

Scottish botanist John Fraser visited the mountain in 1787, giving particular attention to the high elevation northern disjunct forest ecosystem remindful of the few remnants left in the Scots highlands. Fraser put his name on the dominant species of that forest, the Fraser Fir.

Seven years later the Frenchman Andre Michaux labored up to the summit of Grandfather Mountain, and throwing all scientific caution to the winds, pronounced immediately to the world that it was the highest in the entire country. With fine Gallic exuberance, he celebrated his discovery by bellowing out the *Marseillaise,* his country's national anthem, from the summit, or so he claimed.

Michaux had far more to offer the mountain's now lengthy scientific tradition than mere showmanship. He gathered 2,500 specimens of trees, shrubs, and flowers from the area, and cultivated the idea of using upland species like azalea and rhododendron for garden ornamentals. He introduced to the mountains the delicate Oriental flowering tree the mimosa, and many native American flora to Europe. Michaux's son, Francois Andre, continued his work, visiting Grandfather in 1802.

Asa Gray, distinguished Professor of Botany at University of Cambridge (later Harvard), in Massachusetts, took his turn on the mountain in 1841. His goal was a comprehensive plant survey of the eastern United States. Published 9 years later,

*Gray's Manual of Botany* listed all flora east of the Rockies, and is even today considered the definitive study.

Following Gray was Moses Ashley Curtis, working out of the University of North Carolina. Curtis inventoried highland species on the peaks of Roan and Grandfather for his 1860 work, *Geological and Natural History Survey of North Carolina*. He described it, probably accurately, as "a larger list than has yet been published in the Union." Curtis's in-depth research first confirmed the fact that much of the unusual flora growing at the high elevations were disjunct forms that had derived from northern boreal forests and displaced by the ice age.

The Civil War, and the opening of the frontier that followed, put a temporary halt to these empirical investigations. A hundred years would lapse before scientific enquiry returned in earnest to the Grandfather region, and put it back in the forefront of natural history research.

The war made its mark on the mountains, but probably less so than any other region in the South. The Cherokee had been marched out on the Trail of Tears in 1838, with the survivors living, much as the whites, hand to mouth on their reservation in the Great Smokies. The occasional skirmishes and troop movements (there were no full-scale engagements in the North Carolina Blue Ridge) had less impact than the deepening poverty, although mountain people were well used to that.

Except as sanctuary, the high country around Grandfather provided little strategic value, and remained outside the theatre of war. Loyalties in the area were mixed. Very few mountain families owned slaves, though slavery did exist, restricted mainly by lack of land and wealth to create a slave-based economy. Both the high mountains and the mountain residents stubbornly resisted outside influences, and change, whichever side of the spectrum they came from.

The Grandfather Community, the first permanent settlement formed on the mountain since the Melungeons, had been established in 1815, along the Watauga River on the northern slope. Although the first registered landowner was the Revolutionary War hero Captain Lenoir, who was deeded 8,000 acres high on the mountain, the first actual settler was Isaac McCurd, who that year claimed 2,000 acres.

The Scots-Irish families who followed adopted the definitive slow pace of southern mountain living. The first church (Baptist) wasn't built until 1844, the first school until 1869, and the first Post Office (Government!) until 1881. By 1888, only 23 families had settled in the Community, and just another handful along the riversheds of the south side of Grandfather Mountain.

The first scandal rocked the close-knit huddle of log and frame cabins in 1850. One Cob McCandles, son of original settler Jim McCandles, had been appointed Sheriff and Tax Collector, but he couldn't give much of an account of the tax monies turned over to him, which had, in fact, mysteriously disappeared. He was served with a warrant and jailed. His father's good friend Isaac McCurd put his whole 2,000 acre stake up as bail bond. Freed, Cob McCandles promptly retrieved his ill-gotten gains, took a lady friend, and high-tailed it out west. McClurd lost all his land, but McCandles lost his life, in a dispute with no less an eminence than "Wild" Bill Hickock.

The Community produced its first writer, Shepard Dugger, at the outset of the Civil War. Dugger taught in the one-room schoolhouse, and wrote *The Balsam Groves of Grandfather Mountain* in 1860. Equal parts local lore, story, and inspiration, it represented the region's earliest work of literature.

Gold was discovered up the north slope in 1870, and mined for 7 years. Whether with deliberate secrecy or by geographical isolation, or both, word of the strike never set off a frenzied gold rush to the mountain. The mining remained a small-time local affair, panning out steady if unspectacular yield.

The rush came anyway, but had nothing to do with gold. With the Civil War over and the frontier beckoning, not even the remotest corners of the northwest North Carolina could resist what was coming. The eastern cities, filling up to bursting from European emigration, unleashed a flood of people west. Driven by war-generated technological advances; railroad, telegraph, repeating rifle, and dynamite, the American frontier blew open.

The 1880's would launch the modern era onto Grandfather Mountain.

# CHAPTER 6

## *Exploitation*

The great mountain slopes and forests...had been ruinously detimbered; the farm soil on the hillsides had eroded and washed down, high up, upon the hills, one saw the raw scars of old mica pits, the dump heaps of deserted mines...It was evident that a huge compulsive greed had been at work; the whole region had been sucked and gutted, milked dry, denuded of its rich primeval treasures, something blind and ruthless had been here, grasped, and gone. The blind scars on the hills, the denuded slopes, the empty mica pits were what was left...Something had come into the wilderness, and left the barren land.

-- THOMAS WOLFE, *THE HILLS BEYOND*, 1941

Grandfather Mountain is a heritage far too precious to turn over to the exploiter armed with ax and saw to devastate and despoil.

-- HARLAND P. KELSEY, BOTANIST, 1930

The brief prosperity brought on by the bonanza of modernization broadened the mountaineer's economic horizon. It aroused aspirations, envies, and hopes. But the industrial wonders of the age promised more than they in fact delivered, for the profits taken from the rich natural resources of the region flowed out of the mountains, with little benefit to the mountain people themselves. For a relative handful of owners and managers, the new order mountaineers, the new order yielded riches unimaginable a few decades before; for thousands of mountaineers, it brought a life of struggle, hardship, and despair. Considered from this perspective, the persistent poverty of Appalachia has not resulted from the lack of modernization. Rather, it has come from the particular kind of modernization that unfolded in the years 1880 to 1930.

-- U.S. GOVERNMENT SURVEY ON POVERTY IN APPALACHIA, 1967

Tourism is a sort of chemotherapy -- you have cancer and it's the only possible cure, but it might kill you before the cancer does.

-- JUAN ANTONIO BLANCO, HISTORIAN

Work began on the Grandfather Mountain region's first tourist 'attraction' in 1885. Four years later, Shep Dugger, along with Ervin and Texas Bird Calloway, had completed the Grandfather Hotel on the Burnsville Road just below Linville

Gap. It attracted some vacationers to the cool upland summer, but with just one rough road into the region, hardly produced a wave of visitors.

That wave began when the first outside developer, Hugh MacRae of Wilmington, North Carolina, formed the Linville Improvement Company with Samuel Kelsey. MacRae was an industrialist and railroad magnate who not only recognized the potential profits from tourism (and timber), but possessed the wherewithal to realize them.

By 1891 MacRae had established the resort town of Linville at the northeast foot of the mountain. Targeting wealthy flatlanders, he built a toll road, the Yonahlossee Turnpike, between Linville and Blowing Rock. The exclusive Eseeola Inn was completed a year later.

The Linville Improvement Company then purchased additional land, approximately 16,000 acres, that comprised much of Grandfather Mountain. The summits and rugged upper slopes were left undisturbed at the outset, although a rough track was cut up from the turnpike, and a construction foreman reportedly built a home and grazed sheep on what is now MacRae Meadows.

Plenty of 'improvements', on the other hand, were underway in the Linville and Watauga River valleys below. The first order of business was to extract the timber. Initially, this was accomplished by 'donkey train' with the animals pulling carts along rails extending deep into the great tree stands of the mountain's coves. By 1918, the East Tennessee and Western North Carolina (ET&WNC) Railroad extended its narrow gauge track through the Linville Gap, and the taking out of the massive trees began in earnest.

Other trappings of civilization were carried in with the twentieth century. The first newspaper, called *Grandfather Greetings*, rolled off the press in 1910.

The charter of Avery County, the last formed in North Carolina, was drawn up in 1911, from lands previously allocated to Mitchell, Caldwell, and McDowell counties. It encompassed an area, including the bulk of Grandfather, that had been managed by the Cherokee, Melungeons, Spanish,

French, English, the Confederacy, and the United States Government.

By the early 1920's, the railroad and the Linville Improvement Company had completed their work at the base of the mountain, earning the denuded area around Linville the nickname of "Stumptown". Throughout the high country similar conditions prevailed, as other developers grasped opportunities. Resort developments were going up as the trees were coming down, on Beech Mountain, in Boone, Banner Elk, Blowing Rock, and Sugar Mountain. During the twenties, the summer visitors returned yearly, apparently unperturbed by vistas of smoking clear-cuts.

Many of the poorer mountain men of the Grandfather and other communities left their small plots of corn and orchard to cut the trees, and work the mills, hotels, and railroad. With fish, game and other forest bounty now near ground zero, and little actual income from their small farms, they recognized that the old ways of self-sustenance were no longer tenable. One thing didn't change working for the development corporations: the locals stayed poor.

Then came 1929. The Crash and the ensuing Depression hit the rural south hard, and Appalachia hardest of all. Not only had the traditional means of survival been cut away, but the new market economy had collapsed as well. There were cut trees, eroded land, silted rivers, and now, no jobs.

But as they looked up, they could see some forest still still standing, some thousands of acres yet uncut, up on the steep slopes of Grandfather Mountain. The Linville Improvement Company contracted with Will Smith in 1930 to take it all out. Smith had recently completed a similar assignment on Roan Mountain, shipping all the timber off to the largest commercial operation ever in the western part of the state, the Champion Pulp and Paper Mill down in Canton, North Carolina. Some of the last ancient forests in the southeast United States were going to be taken for pulp.

The desperate unemployed lined up to take them down.

Eight miles of plank roads were constructed to haul the timber off the mountain and onto waiting freight cars bound for

Canton. By 1933 the north side of the mountain had been stripped near to the stone, and three more years would account for the south slope as well. The stumps were burnt off, and the workers left them smoldering and headed home, unemployed again.

On Grandfather, briars and chokeberries grew.

The rains began on August 10, 1940, and lasted three full days. The cut out, washed out mountain couldn't hold the torrent, and massive mud slides rampaged into the Grandfather Community and other settlements, destroying most of its houses, barns, and crops, even the railroad.

The improvements were concluded. There was nothing left.

# CHAPTER 7

## *Preservation*

Most mountaineers packed up and headed for wartime jobs in Knoxville and Detroit. They left behind less than ten families, fewer than had clutched the hollers two hundred years before, and a silent, nearly lifeless, Grandfather Mountain.

Unhappily, this scenario was hardly limited to the High Country or to southern Appalachia; the century and a half of American expansion had reduced much of the continent to similar conditions.

All but tiny remnants of the vast eastern forest had fallen to the axe and saw. Destroyed with it was a diversity and concentration of wildlife unmatched in any temperate clime of the planet. In 1743, deliveries from the New World to a single French seaport included 127,080 beaver, 30,325 marten, 12,428 otter and fisher, 110,000 raccoon, and 16,512 bear pelts. In 1735, the Cherokee alone sold a million deerskins. In 1796, a single trading party from Charleston, South Carolina brought out 30 wagon loads of animal skins from the mountains.

The woods bison that traveled in great herds through their forest habitat was eliminated everywhere east of the Appalachians by 1801. The last animal was shot in Pennsylvania, by whatever providential design, at a place called Buffalo Cross Roads.

The last elk was taken out, also in Pennsylvania, in 1867; the last Caribou in Maine in 1905, the same year the last gray wolf of the east went down in North Carolina. The year 1903 heralded the end of the eastern cougar everywhere outside corners of Appalachia and the Florida Everglades.

The final sighting in the wild of the Carolina Parakeet, the only native North American parrot, came at Florida's Lake Okeechobee in 1904. Ten years later the last bird died in captivity. That year too spelled the end of the Passenger pigeon, reduced from flocks totaling tens, maybe hundreds of millions, to one bird dead in a cage at the Cincinnati Zoo.

During the Depression, much of Appalachia participated in "vermin campaigns", a series of mass kill-offs organized by sportsmen's groups and often, state 'conservation' departments. Hunters were awarded credit points for each kill, depending on the species. The targeted species were all labeled predators, so called, including such notorious culprits as the hellbender and kingfisher. A golden eagle fetched the most points, followed by goshawks, broadwings, redtails, sparrow hawks, and all carnivorous mammals.

One year the grand prize for most points was a four-year college scholarship, awarded to a young man who had killed eleven nesting goshawks.

Notable among the hundreds of species that barely survived the holocaust were beaver, fisher, otter, fox, and black bear; raven, peregrine, bald and golden eagle, Weller's salamander, hellbender, and ginseng. Animal bounties had, in fact, been levied on many species, especially raptors and reptiles, since the very earliest days of colonization. As early as 1697, in New Jersey, a dead grey wolf brought ten shillings to a Negro or Indian, twice that to a "Christian" hunter.

Despite Lawson's caution twenty years later that wolves did not kill humans, the bounties continued, and still do.

The 1940's spelled the end for the American chestnut and the ivory-billed woodpecker. First noted by John Lawson back in Carolina in 1711, the ivory-billed was the largest and most striking woodpecker of the Americas. Two hundred years later, hunted and driven from habitat, it was thought to be extinct, but a few birds were spotted in their last redoubt of the Louisiana marsh country in 1946. They were cornered in a stand of virgin cypress, which they required for nesting, and an appeal made to the timber company to stop cutting the last of these trees. They refused, and the bird was considered by the 1970's to be completely extirpated.

The American chestnut was once the dominant tree of the east, accounting for up to 40% of all species in the hardwood forests. The virus that caused the Chestnut Blight had crossed into New York from Europe in the early 1900's, and spread with such fury that only forty years later the entire population, over an area of tens of thousands of square miles, had died and would not reseed.

Compounding the problems of overhunting and habitat destruction, this extinguishing of such a widespread species perfectly illustrates how extensive was the mayhem caused by introduction, both accidental and deliberate, of non-native species.

In the Great Smoky Mountains, the European wild boar was introduced for sport hunting in the 1920's, escaped from the hunting preserves, and has been wreaking havoc on endemic flora ever since. During the same period, stocking of docile farmed trout drove the native Appalachian brook trout to the highest reaches of the remotest headwaters, and to the brink of extinction.

The scope of the damage prompted an outcry and a strong response; the formation of a national conservation movement, both inside and outside government. One of the earliest countermeasures, an attempt to reintroduce an extirpated species to its original range, occurred along the lower reaches of Grandfather Mountain.

Although the motive may have been less ecological than the desire to propagate fine hunting specimens, the first species reintroduction in the United States brought one hundred elk from Yellowstone Park to Grandfather in 1917. Shipped in a wagon train of rolling cages, the animals were released willy-nilly around the mountain and the region. No steps had been taken to prepare them for the wild, nor to alert the residents of nearby mountain communities. As a result, the elk roamed hungrily into local gardens, orchards and homesteads, where they were destroyed by puzzled and annoyed farmers.

However misguided, this effort demonstrated the growing concern for America's disappearing wild grandeur and the formation of an organized campaign to save it. Inspired in large part by the work of Lawson, Catesby and Bartram in North Carolina, America produced in her time of need a line of prominent writer/naturalist/preservationists unmatched in history; J.J. Audubon, Alexander Wilson, Henry David Thoreau, Ralph Emerson, Horace Greeley, John Muir, who visited Grandfather Mountain, and Frederick Law Olmstead, to name just a few. Their efforts in turn established conservation as a national priority, reflected in the most far-reaching legislation ever undertaken to protect a nation's natural heritage; the creation of the National Park System in 1872. That year Yellowstone National Park was founded in the wilds of Wyoming; Yosemite and Sequoia followed in California in 1890. Four years later the concept was expanded to promote a series of federally protected preserves, the first in the world, by the Park Protection Act of 1894.

A managing federal agency, the National Park Service, was created in 1916 "to conserve the scenery and the natural and historic objects and the wildlife therein, and to provide for the enjoyment of same in such manner and by such means as will leave them unimpaired for the enjoyment of future generations."

In 1916, it was no mean feat to find many 'natural objects unimpaired', or much 'wildlife therein'. But under their mandate for future preservation, the National Park Service could look beyond current conditions to protecting and restoring some vestige of the great wilderness.

Where to look? With large parks already established in the west, the logical decision followed to create a preserve east of the Rockies, of enough size and integrity to justify its purchase with large amounts of taxpayer's money.

The United States Geological Survey had first surveyed Grandfather Mountain in 1903. The road to the summit had been improved (and a toll levied), and if Linville was being timbered relentlessly, the mountain proper remained at this stage relatively intact. Championed by botanist Harland Kelsey, the area's first and foremost environmentalist, Grandfather Mountain became the leading candidate for the site of a Blue Ridge National Park, to be preserved forever.

In 1918, the Civil Services Act authorized the Secretary of the Interior to "accept for park purposes any lands and right of ways, including the Grandfather Mountain, near or adjacent to the government forest reserve in Western North Carolina." This existing reserve referred to land belonging to the U.S. Forest Service. The Forest Service had been established under the auspices of President Theodore Roosevelt in 1901. Headed by the sometime conservationist Gifford Pinchot, the Forest Service had already purchased thousands of acres from private holdings below Linville Improvement Company land on the sweeping south slope of the mountain.

Pinchot perfectly mirrored the dichotomy of the times regarding the nation's wild heritage. Pinchot believed the remaining wilderness could be utilized and preserved at the same time. He developed the concept of 'multiple-use' on Forest Service tracts, whereby the land was set aside to satisfy a variety of interests, or special interests. The Forest Service consequently turned their holdings into an assortment of recreation areas, strip mines, cattle ranches, wilderness pockets and clear-cuts, patched together to try and satisfy two definitions of usefulness; economics and recreation.

More than seventy years would pass before the real owners of the land, United States citizens, would utilize the forests in such numbers to spotlight this juggling act; and put on the front pages the debate whether multiple-use was a workable compromise or an unmanageable fumble of contradictions. The Park Service, on the other hand, was bound by its founding charter to adhere to, especially in the context of the early 20th century, very stringent standards of protection. As the Forest Service was proceeding with multiple use policy along the Wilson's Creek watershed, i.e. cutting down trees, Park Service officials looked to the Linville Improvement Company to sell them their holdings as the basis for the new park.

With a willing buyer and willing seller, Kelsey anticipated a straightforward deal, but from the outset negotiations became entangled in what constituted the value of the land. The Improvement Company wanted to include the timber value in the asking price, and intimated they would start cutting the trees if the Park Service did not raise their offer. As a public agency, the Service funds were limited, and they could not hope to match what they considered a grossly inflated price.

Kelsey worked tirelessly, forsaking his business and all other interests to consummate the deal. But the owners wouldn't budge, and with coffers further depleted from World War I, the Federal Government began to look elsewhere for their park. Kelsey then lobbied state officials, hoping to work a last-minute deal to create North Carolina's first state park, anything to preserve the mountain.

By the 1930's, the trees were indeed being brought down on Grandfather Mountain. Kelsey continued to labor on for another ten years to put Grandfather into public ownership. North Carolina state officials did come to the table with an offer to buy the land for a Grandfather Mountain State Park, but here too, an agreement on price could not be reached.

Meanwhile the Park Service successfully created their first regional preserve, the Great Smoky Mountains National Park, along the North Carolina-Tennessee boundary.

The Smokies were authorized on May 22, 1926, established for administration and protection on February 6, 1930, and established for full development on June 15, 1934.

Another federal project, however, one unique in the world, would ultimately conjoin the Parks agency and Grandfather Mountain. The Blue Ridge Parkway was one of the many visionary notions to spring from the Roosevelt administration out of the desperate reality of the Depression. The Park Service planned to construct a linear national park, served by a single road, that would traverse no fewer than five mountain ranges in the Appalachian Mountain chain.

Despite taking out plenty of trees, the Parkway would protect the crest of the Blue Ridge from being totally timbered again just as the mountains were beginning to recover from the clear-cutting of the 19th century. Its construction would bring not only preservation, but employment along the length of Appalachia. It would open up the region to the rest of the nation, bringing, it was hoped, prosperity at long last.

The Blue Ridge Parkway represented classic New Deal legislation -- opportunistic, costly, and above all, controversial. Some Congressional opponents were beside themselves; "...the most gigantic and stupendously extravagant and unreasonable expenditure by the most extravagantly expensive administration in the history of the world," according to one Republican legislator.

Funded nevertheless, construction began September 11, 1935, with a view to connecting Shenandoah National Park above Front Royal, Va., with the Great Smoky Mountains.

By the time the road had dipped and turned three hundred miles to the slopes of the Grandfather, everything seemed ready to incorporate the greatest of the Blue Ridge Mountains into America's first publicly owned parkway.

To be sure, World War II had siphoned off men, materiel, and money, and even after the war, federal funding remained scarce. But the National Park Service had in the interim managed to purchase 7,500 acres of land on the mountain, already clear-cut, from the Linville Improvement Company. All in all, the Park Service, working through the states of North Carolina and Virginia, had successfully negotiated terms with 4,000 private landowners, working out rights of way, easements, or condemnation to assure the Parkway's completion.

By 1950 two very generous donations had already enhanced the scenic and preservation value of the operation; a gift of the 3,600 acre estate of North Carolina textile giant Moses Cone, and 4,000 acres donated from the estate of Jefferson Standard Life Assurance founder Julian Price, one of the state's greatest philanthropists. These beautiful lands spreading at the northern base of Grandfather Mountain greatly broadened the traditionally narrow perimeters of the Parkway, and were to prove as great attractions as the Grandfather itself.

But trouble was brewing again on the mountain. By the early 1950's, the Blue Ridge Parkway had been completed along its entire 469 mile route except for a small portion on the south shoulder owned by the Linville Improvement Company. The Company dissolved in 1952, with ownership of their lands reverting to a single heir, McCrae's grandson, Hugh Morton. While Kelsey was still trying in vain to negotiate a larger agreement to create a national or state park, Morton and Parkway officials disagreed over the exact route of this final segment, a dispute that would prevent its completion for over 15 years.

The postwar economic boom had by this time returned the summer visitors to the region, opened up by the Parkway and other roads, and Morton constructed a profitable tourist attraction on the summit, Grandfather Mountain Incorporated. By the 1960's, with resort growth throughout the high country booming, Morton co-founded the Wilmor Development Corporation, which would later build a country club and second home resort along almost two thousand acres of the north slope.

Further development was challenged by environmentalists, and ultimately some of the land was protected.

The disagreement with the Parkway was resolved in 1975, when Park Service officials created a masterful design to swing the road around the sheer slope and rock outcropping that had hindered the last segment. They engineered the Linn Cove Viaduct, constructed in pre-cast blocks that followed the contour of the slope and could be completed, from the existing road and from the air, without dynamite and with minimal environmental impact.

Much as earlier degradations had engendered the conservation movement of the early 20th century, so too did rampant growth and development after the War, in the High Country Region as throughout scenic America, produce a defining controversy of the century's latter half: land use management.

As late as the 1920's, there had been more than enough land to go around. Deeds had actually been given away as premiums with boxes of soap, and as incentives for newspaper subscriptions.

But with substantial government purchases, and extensive ownership by development corporations in the years since, questions necessarily arose whether, and how, and who will be appointed to manage an obviously finite 'resource'.

Through the 1960's and 1970's the development of land on and around the mountain went largely or at least publicly unquestioned; the efforts to turn Grandfather into a federally or state-protected park were in the past and the future seemed to belong to the tourism industry.

Grandfather Mountain Incorporated, i.e. the tourist attraction on the summit, the Country Club, the toney "Shoppes" at the base, were accepted as revenue-makers in an area that always had to balance natural beauty and survival. By the 1980's this kind of compromise was becoming a harder line to justify in those natural areas that were irreplaceable, and also attractions in their own right. Scientific evidence of rare and endangered plant and animal communities and the growing industry of eco-tourism were beginning to demand fuller protection for their own sake and also for human enjoyment.

The perception now was that incremental development -- the death of a thousand cuts -- presented just as much a danger to the visiting neo-tropical songbird or groups of trout fisherman as the wholesale destruction of massive deforestation or heavy industry.

In 1988 the debate reached critical mass on the most critical place in the High Country: Grandfather Mountain's North Slope. The Wilmor Corporation planned to develop (or sell the development package) most of the remaining wild and unprotected land on this side of the mountain, and build a ski resort, condos, houses, shopping centers, et al. The uproar was immediate, and lasted almost five years, as the issues of property rights, Hugh Morton's (a one-third partner in Wilmor) good name and good works, conservation and community came and stayed to the fore.

One group, Friends of Grandfather Mountain, kept the issue and the protection efforts alive with a hard line drawn on the North Slope, claiming it was a proven treasure trove for rare, threatened, and endangered species, and too important to allow any intrusion. The compromise solution that eventually saved 600 acres and allowed building on 300 more was generally lauded as another of Morton's (and the North Carolina Nature Conservancy's) steps to preserve the mountain.

Unfortunately the land that was taken included one of the oldest hiking trails in the South -- the Shanty Springs Trail -- land adjoining The Glade, and the headwaters to the Linville and

Watauga Rivers. When the development was begun for a supermarket, fast food outlets, motels and condos, heavy rains from Hurricane Opal washed out insufficient holding ponds and silted the pristine upper Watauga for twenty miles.

Construction was stopped temporarily, fines levied, and many of the companies planning to build abandoned the project in the ensuing controversy.

Morton fiercely defended his rights on his own land and his preservation record. His critics called him hypocritical and more concerned with image than substantial efforts to completely protect his portion of Grandfather Mountain. Morton tried to find a middle ground by developing some areas while donating others -- amounting to thousands of acres -- to preservation groups like the North Carolina Nature Conservancy.

The issue is not going away any time soon: each year the land becomes more valuable, both as legacy and property.

In a study of mountain land issues in 1974, a University of Tennessee report stated:

> To most Americans, development is synonymous with progress. The recent land boom in recreational real estate is similar to earlier land booms in American history, fueled by speculative demand. Nineteenth and twentieth were for commercial and residential use, the latest is for recreational.

The region around Grandfather Mountain provided fertile ground for this type of development, providing cheap land, a poor, disenfranchised local population, and few if any land-use regulations. Ski resorts, golf courses, vacation homes, and strip malls sprang up in Banner Elk, Foscoe, and on the North Slope of Grandfather himself.

The unrestrained building kept pace with such growth nationwide. The University of Tennessee report continues: "large land corporations typically buy a huge plot, bulldoze a few roads, dig out an artificial lake or build a golf course, and sell lots to the public."

These are precisely the steps taken by Grandfather Golf and Country Club and many other resorts around the mountain.

Mountain people, including some few holdouts from the original Grandfather Community, faced the choice of holding on to the family plot that generated no income beyond subsistence, or sell to outside interests and either leave the area or apply for poorly paid jobs at the new resort. Many sold. By 1993, the number of families living in the Grandfather Community had dwindled to only four.

According to the report, unlike planned urban or suburban communities,

> The ease with which developers operate in rural areas is partially the result of both attitudes and conditions often found in these regions...without any controls governing the location, size, and quality of development, decisions on these factors are often made primarily by the developer for his benefit.

Not only much of the community, but much of the profits from recreational development end up leaving the region. Soaring taxes, inflated land prices, and poverty remain. Land prices at development areas on and around Grandfather Mountain have been known to rise at four hundred percent annually.

Part of the problem is that land sold in this speculative manner frequently never results in a house being built, denying the labor, income and tax base it would generate. In 1971, the National Association of Home Builders estimated that 10,000 developers had sold 650,000 recreational lots nationwide, but only 95,000 vacation homes were actually constructed. The land then sits or changes hands at ever higher prices, with no benefit to the community. One three hundred acre parcel at the base of Grandfather Mountain was purchased from the family owners for $30,000. Less than one hundred acres of this land was then resold for a subdivision, for $156,000.

Out of the sold price of each resort lot, on the average, one-third covers the cost of the land and its improvements, one-third covers the cost of promotion, and one-third is profit, one of the highest margins of any industry. This does not include the bonuses attached to financing, club memberships, or in construction.

In the 1960's, lots at the Grandfather Golf and Country Club sold for $20,000 to $30,000 per acre. Country club membership (mandatory) cost $6,500 plus $600 annual dues, and construction of a new house from $80,000 to $250,000.

As late as 1974, Avery County had no zoning or subdivision regulations, nor even required building permits. At one point, 8,000 lots had been bulldozed, but only 1000 dwellings erected. One of those structures put an end forever to unrestricted growth in the North Carolina mountains.

Across the Watauga River valley from Grandfather's north slope stands Sugar Mountain, a prominent peak exceeding 5,000 feet.

It has recently become more prominent still, sprouting a ten-story condominium, called Sugartop, on the summit. All too visible from Grandfather Mountain and most other vantage points, this intrusion proved too much for residents and developers alike, who were after all, trying to sell not only the bulk but also the idea of a beautiful mountain region. Swayed by unified regional pressure, including strong efforts from Hugh Morton and Grandfather Mountain, Inc., the North Carolina Legislature subsequently passed a Ridge Top Law, banning future construction of multi-story buildings on any ridge in the state.

Development certainly did not stop or even slow appreciably, but the idea of controls, however minimal and overdue, had at last been introduced. More would follow.

By the 1990's, complex concepts like sustainable development, bio-regions, and micro-habitats had become part of public environmental debate, and conservation issues taken to the heart of what will be the future of mountain culture, communities, ecosystems, and wildlife.

What will be the future of Grandfather Mountain?

The mountain admits many perspectives in many realms. On the ground Grandfather has been spared a Sugartop, but not the scattershot development that is now known to destroy ecological and visual integrity. Once complete, then devastated, the natural systems have restored themselves to a degree, to what degree we have insufficient knowledge to assess. Is the glass now half-full or half-empty? What damage is irreversible?

Historically, Grandfather is a survivor, so venerable in time that a few seconds of human activity might not make the final, or even a lasting, determination, on Grandfather Mountain.

This does not mean we can afford to return to the manifest destiny of past centuries, past decades, where we impose our will regardless of the consequences. For the sake of our children we must acknowledge the effects our presence will have on the mountain for lifetimes to come. Like all that has gone before, fire, ice, stone, plant, animal and human, all of us setting foot on the mountain play a role in what will follow in these footsteps.

Conversely, Grandfather belongs to all of us. This is what Dr. Hight C. Moore, visitor from Nashville, Tennessee, took home one day fifty years ago:

> Grandfather is akin to you and looks lovingly down upon you; welcomes you, entertains in high-peak style; yet himself sits or reclines at the head of the table and sleeps alone in his own big bed. He is a sovereign at ease in a splendid court, his serenity matched only by his supremacy.
>
> He is your Grandfather.

# Bibliography

Adkins, Leonard, *Walking the Blue Ridge* (Chapel Hill: UNC Press, 1991).

Alexander, William C., *An Avifaunal Strip Census on Grandfather Mountain* (Boone: 1970)

Britten, Nathaniel Lord, *Illustrated Flora of the Northern U.S. and Canada.*

Brooks, Maurice, *The Appalachians* (Boston: Houghton Mifflin, 1965).

Catesby, Mark, *Natural History of the Carolinas* (1731).

Catlin, David T., *A Naturalist's Blue Ridge Parkway* (Knoxville: University of Tennessee Press, 1984).

Eifert, Virginia, *Men, Birds, and Adventure* (New York: Dodd, Mead & Co., 1962).

Elman, Robert, *First in the Field* (New York: Mason/Charter, 1977).

Faragher, John Mack, *Daniel Boone* (New York: Holt & Co., 1992).

Fox, Stephen, *The American Conservation Movement* (New York: Little, Brown & Co., 1981).

Gray, Asa, *Manual of Botany.*

Hanley, Wayne, *Natural History in America* (New York: Demeter Press, 1977).

Harper, Francis, Ed., *Travels of William Bartram* (New Haven: Yale University Press, 1958).

Horton, James; Perdue, Theda; Gifford, James, *Our Mountain Heritage* (Cullowhee: Western Carolina University, 1979).

Kelsey, Harlan P., *Flora of Grandfather Mountain* (East Boxford, Massachusetts).

Lanham, Charles, *Letters From the Alleghany Mountain.*

Lawson, John, *History of North Carolina* (1711).

Matthiessen, Peter, *Wildlife in America* (New York: Viking, 1959, 1987).

Peck, Rodney, *Indian Projectile Point Types from Virginia and the Carolinas* (Harrisburg, North Carolina, 1982).

Purrington, Bert, *Prehistory of North Carolina.*

Raymond, Loren, *Glacial, Periglacial, and Pseudo-Glacial Features in the Grandfather Mountain Area* (Durham, North Carolina: Duke University, 1977).

Sutton, Ann and Myron, Eds., *Eastern Forests*, Audubon Society Nature Guide (New York: Knopf, 1985).

# Index

## A

Abbey, Edward 81
Acidic Cove Forest 22
Adirondack Glaciation 6
Agriculture, Native American 59
Alexander County, North Carolina
    66
Alleghenian Orogeny 2
Animals, Captive Breeding of 37
Appalachian Brook Trout 27
Appalachian Mountain Range
    11, 71
Appalachian Summit Region 54
Appalachian Woodlands 13
Ashe County, North Carolina
    11, 56, 69
Attic Window 18, 58
Audubon, John J. 80, 92
Avery County, North Carolina
    11, 69, 86
Azalea, Flame 81

## B

Balsam Mountains 67
Banner Elk, North Carolina
    37, 87, 98
Bartram, William 31, 80, 82
Bats, Virginia Big-Eared 41
Bears 35
Beech Mountain, North Carolina 87
Bent Avens 19, 25
Bering Strait 79
Birds, Theory of Migration of 79
Black Cherry 21
Black Rock Cliffs Cave 41
Blanco, Juan Antonio 85
Blowing Rock, North Carolina 87
Blue Ridge Mountains 11, 80
Blue Ridge National Park 92
Blue Ridge Parkway 94

Boone, Daniel 73
Boone Fork Rock Shelter 56
Boone, North Carolina 71, 76, 87
Boone, Rebecca 74
Boone's Fork 73
Boonesborough, Kentucky 73
Burnsville, North Carolina
    60, 75, 76

## C

Caldwell County, North Carolina
    86
Calloway, Ervin and Texas Bird 85
Calloway's Peak 18
Catawba Indians 61, 66
Catawba River 27
Catesby, Mark 79
Champion Pulp and Paper Mill
    Company 87
Chapel Hill, North Carolina 71
Cherokee Indians 60, 75
    Hunting 62
    Life and Customs 62
    Mythology 62, 63, 65
        Quartz Crystals 64
    Trail of Tears 75, 83
Cherry, Black 21
Chestnut Blight 26, 90
Chimney Rock Park 50
Collins, Vandy 70
Cornell University Ornithology
    Laboratory 50
Cottontail, Eastern 40
Cougars 36
Cove Creek, North Carolina 56
Craggy Gardens 20
Cranberry Gneiss 4
Crossnore, North Carolina 36
Currituck Sound, North Carolina 78
Curtis, Moses Ashley 83

## D

Darwin, Charles 76
De Soto, Hernando 60, 67

Deales Museum, Philadelphia 81
Dugger, Shepard 84, 85
Dunn, Dr. Emmet R. 30

E

Elizabethton, Tennessee 69
Elk, North American 38
Emerson, Ralph 92
*Ericaceae 20*
Eseeola Inn 86
Estatoe, Chief 75
ET&WNC Railroad 86

F

Falcons 49
Flame Azalea 81
Foscoe, North Carolina 98
Franklin, Benjamin 81
Franklin, North Carolina 67
Fraser Fir 82
Fraser, John 31, 82
Friends of Grandfather Mountain,
    The 97

G

Galax 26
Glaciation, Adirondack 6
Glade, The 24, 46, 97
Gneiss 3, 4, 57, 65
Grandfather Community
    83, 87, 88, 98
Grandfather Golf and Country Club
    97, 98, 99
*Grandfather Greetings* 86
Grandfather Hotel 85
Grandfather Mountain
    1722 Expedition 80
    Agriculture 59
    Attic Window 18
    Calloway's Peak 18
    Climate 13
    Ecosystems 11, 15
        Acidic Cove Forest 22
        Aquatic Habitat 27

Habitats 15
    Mixed Forests 25
    Northern Hardwood Forest 21
    Rich Cove Forest 22, 24
    Spruce-Fir Ecosystem 20
    Subalpine Environment 16
Fauna
    Appalachian Brook Trout 27
    Bears 34
    Birds 42
    Cottontail, Eastern 40
    Cougars 37
    Falcons 49
    Freshwater Mussels 28
    Mammals 33
    Mountain Lion 36
    Mouse, Golden 40
    Northern Flying Squirrel 38
    Owls 46
    Ravens 47
    Red Wolf 37
    Reptiles 32
    River Otters 38
    Salamanders 28
    Warblers 45
    Weasel, Least 40
Flora
    Flowering Plants 18, 24
    Heath Balds 20
    Lichen 17
    Mosses 17
    Trees 12, 21
Geological Survey 92
History
    Birth of 1
    Cenozoic Era 7
    Civil War Period 83
    Pleistocene Era 5
Inhabitants
    Melungeons 68
    Prehistoric Human Activity 53
    Scots-Irish Settlers 71
    Settlers 69
Land Deeds 75
Location and size 7

Minerals 8
Profile Cliffs 50
Quartz Deposits 4
Real Estate 99
Rivers 27
Settler-Indian Conflict 70
Grandfather Mountain Incorporated
  96, 97
Grandfather Mountain State Park
  94
Grandfather Window 3, 16
Gray, Asa 31, 82
Great Depression 87
Great Smoky Mountains
  12, 23, 91, 95
  National Park 94
Greeley, Horace 92

### H

Hawksbill Mountain 50
Heath Balds 20
Hickock, "Wild" Bill 84
High Point, North Carolina 78
Hopewell Mounds 58
Hopewellian Culture 60

### I

Indian Rocks Cave 58

### J

Jefferson, Thomas 81
Julian Price Park 32, 50, 58, 95

### K

Kelsey, Harland 19, 85, 92, 93, 95
Kelsey, Samuel 86

### L

Lawson, John 31, 77, 90
Lee, David 45
Lees-McRae College 37
Lenoir, Captain 83
Lincoln, Abraham 74

Lincoln, Thomas and Nancy 74
Linn Cove Viaduct 41, 96
Linnaeus, Carolus 78
Linville, Charles 70, 75
Linville Falls 4
Linville Falls Fault 5
Linville Gap 71, 76, 85, 86
Linville Improvement Company
  86, 87, 93, 95
Linville, North Carolina 58, 86
Linville River 27, 32, 97
Linville River Gorge 5
Linville Watershed 55
Little Grassy Creek 25

### M

MacRae, Hugh 86
MacRae Meadows 86
Mammals 33
Matthiessen, Peter 36, 44
McCandles, Cob 84
McCurd, Isaac 84
McDowell County, North Carolina
  86
Melungeons 68
Michaux, Andre 12, 26, 31, 82
Michaux, Francois 82
Mississippian Period 60
Mitchell County, North Carolina
  8, 11, 58, 86
Moore, Dr. Hight C. 101
Morton, Hugh 95, 97, 98, 100
Moses Cone Park 32, 95
Mount Mitchell, North Carolina
  11, 20
Mountain Lion 36
Mouse, Golden 40
Muir, John 92

### N

National Park Service 93, 95
National Park System 92
Native Americans
  Agriculture 59

Catawba Indians 61, 65
Cherokee Indians 60, 75
    Hunting 62
    Life and Customs 62
    Mythology 62, 63, 65
Iroquois Indians 61
Tools and Weapons 57
Natural Resources, Destruction of
    89
New Deal Legislation 94
New River, North Fork of 27
Non-Native Species, Introduction of
    91
North American Ice Age 5
North Carolina High Country 11
North Carolina Natural Heritage
    Program 16, 25, 39
North Carolina Nature Conservancy
    25, 97, 98
North Carolina Survey 78
North Carolina Wildlife
    Commission 27
North Slope 98
North Toe River 27
Northern Flying Squirrel 38

**O**

Ohio River Valley (Hopewellian)
    Culture 60
Old Fort, North Carolina 70
Olmstead, Frederick Law 92
Opal, Hurricane 98
Owls 46

**P**

Paleo-Indians
    Archaic Era 56
    Origins 54
    Tools 55
Paleozoic era 1
Paracelcus, Philippus 31
Parris Island, South Carolina 68
Penland, North Carolina 36
Pigeon River Bluffs 50

Pinchot, Gifford 93
Pisgah Culture 61
*Plethodontidae 29*
Plott Balsam Range 45
Precambrian Era 1
Price Lake 50
Profile Cliffs 50
Profile Rock 24
Proto-Cherokee 56, 60

**Q**

Quartz 4, 64, 65
Quartz, Rutilated 65

**R**

Ravens 47
Red Wolf 37
Rich Cove Forest 22, 24
Ridge Top Law 100
River Otters 38
Roan Mountain 2, 16, 17, 45, 87
    Heath Balds 20
Roosevelt, Theodore 93

**S**

Salamanders 28
Scots-Irish Settlers 69, 71
Sequoia National Park 92
Shanty Springs Branch 24
Shanty Springs Trail 46, 97
Shenandoah National Park 95
Shull's Mill 75
Sims Creek and Pond 50
Smith, Will 87
Snakes 32
Snowshoe Hare 40
Spiders 42
Spruce Pine, North Carolina 8
Sugar Mountain 87, 100
Sugartop 100

**T**

Tanawha Trail 3
Tarantula, Spruce-Fir 42

Thoreau, Henry David 92
Trail of Tears 75, 83
Trees 71
Trout, Appalachian Brook 27

## U

U.S. Fish & Wildlife Service 42
U.S. Forest Service 93
Unicoi Mountains 17, 45
University of Tennessee 98

## V

Vermin Campaigns 90

## W

Warblers 45
Watauga County, North Carolina
     11, 69
Watauga River
     27, 28, 56, 71, 73, 76, 83, 86, 98
Watauga River Valley 56
Watauga, Tennessee 69
Watauga Watershed 55, 58
Weasel, Least 40
Weller, Worth Hamilton 30
Whitesides Mountains 50
Wilmor Development Corporation
     96, 97
Wilson, Alexander 81, 92
Wilson Creek Gneiss 3
Wilson's Creek
     3, 27, 47, 55, 58, 93
Wolfe, Thomas 85
Woodland Period Settlements 59

## Y

Yadkin River 27, 73
Yancey County, North Carolina 69
Yellowstone National Park 91, 92
Yonahlossee Road (Turnpike)
     30, 86
Yosemite National Park 92